MEXICO CITY

250 m

TULPETLAC

STA MARIA
TULPETLAC

Mexicable
Estación

CD AZTECA
1RA SECC

Ciénaga
San Jua

SANTA CLARA
COATITLA

Deportivo
Caracoles

Multiplaza
Aragón

GRANJAS VALLE
DE GUADALUPE

NUEVA ARAGÓN

Parque Nacional
El Tepeyac

Parque Ecológico
Lago de Texcoco

Mercado San
Felipe de Jesús

de Santa
Guadalupe

Facultad de
Estudios Superiores

BOSQUE
DE ARAGÓN

Zoológico San
Juan de Aragón

ACUITLAPILCO

CD LAGO

Zócalo

Alameda
Oriente

Aeropuerto Internacional
de la Ciudad
de México

Teatro Acolmixtli
Nezahualcoyotl

EL SOL

Colonia
Gustavo
Baz Prada

XOCHIACA

Plaza
Chimalhuacán

JARDÍN
BALBUENA

AGRÍCOLA
PANTITLÁN

AGUA AZUL

REY NEZA

Autódromo
Hermanos Rodríguez

Rodeo Textcoco

SAN VICENTE
CHICOLOAPAN DE
JUÁREZ CENTRO

Zoológico Parque
del Pueblo

TA CRUZ

LA PERLA

Jardín la Paz
Panteón Privado

Mónumento
Cabeza de Juárez

Unidad
Acaquilpan

CUADRÓN 201

Parque
Cuitláhuac

Universidad
Autónoma
Metropolitana

SANTA MARTHA
ACATITLA

LOS REYES

Deportivo
Soraya Jiménez

IZTAPALAPA

STA MARÍA
AZTAHUACAN

SAN MIGUEL
TEOTONGO

Ampliación
6 de Junio

Parque Luis
Echeverría

LOS ÁNGELES

CULHUACAN

REFORMA
POLÍTICA

Volcán
Xaltepec

AYOTLA

Santa Catarina
Yecahuitzotl

Metro
Nopalera

ANJAS COAPA

Bosque de
Tláhuac

Valle de Chalco
Solidaridad

AMP. SELENE

MEXICO CITY

THE EXTRAORDINARY GUIDES

MEXICO CITY

THIBAUT MOMMALIER | FRANCK JUERY

RIZZOLI UNIVERSE

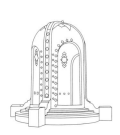
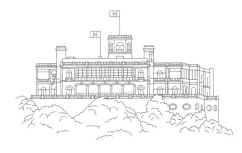
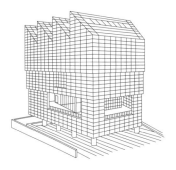

INTRODUCTION

Mexico City may be chaotic but it functions extraordinarily well. The country's capital is home to more than twenty-two million inhabitants and lies at the center of the most highly populated urban agglomeration in the Americas. There was little to suggest, however, that the area surrounding Lake Texcoco, perched at an elevation of 7,875ft (2,400m) and ringed by volcanoes, would one day become the economic, cultural, and culinary heart of an entire continent. Before the Spanish Conquest, the *altepetl* (the city-state founded by the Aztecs in 1325) was known as Tenochtitlan, but once occupied by Hernán Cortés in 1521 it would go on to become México, the capital of New Spain. Mexico declared its independence on September 27, 1821, heralding the start of a succession of empires and dictatorships that included the rule of General Porfirio Díaz before ultimately culminating in a revolution led by Emiliano Zapata and Francisco "Pancho" Villa.

Mexico City is vibrant, and literally so; the city is regularly shaken by destructive earthquakes. The tremor of September 19, 1985 partially razed it to the ground and thirty-two years later to the day (September 19, 2017) a new quake came as a reminder to *Chilangos* (as the inhabitants of Mexico City are known) that nature reigns supreme, even in the middle of this concrete jungle. In 2010 UNESCO recognized Mexican cuisine as Intangible Cultural Heritage and wherever you are in the city, and at any hour of the day, you will find something to eat; small food stands (*puestitos*) are located at the corner of every street.

The architecture of some districts is reminiscent of European capitals, even if ultra-modern skyscrapers rub shoulders with shanty towns and there is a juxtaposition of extremes wherever you look. Mexico City has undergone a historic revival since the turn of the 2000s, however, with the French magazine *L'Obs* even dubbing it the "new global capital of cool" in 2019. Millennials are drawn to it, and both artists and entrepreneurs choose to settle in the city for its quality of life. This megacity might seem like a monster, but if you have the courage to take it on, your reward will be a place at a table that is one of the most joyful, and abundant, in the world.

AN ICON OF A COUNTRY IN CONSTANT TRANSFORMATION

CENTRO HISTÓRICO

Before the Spanish Conquest, the area was known in Nahuatl as *atlepetl*,
the "heart of the town." Since 1980, it has been officially called the
Centro Histórico de la Ciudad de México.

P. 8

Millions of Mexicans visit the Calle Francisco I. Madero every weekend.

OPPOSITE

Mexicans are the biggest consumers of sodas in the world.

This is the largest historic city center in Latin America and one of the world's great concentrations of UNESCO World Heritage-listed buildings, including the ruins of the Aztec Templo Mayor, the Palacio de Bellas Artes, and the Sagrario Metropolitano next door to Mexico City Metropolitan Cathedral.

The district has experienced the best and the worst of the city's history. Every weekend, more than two million bargain hunters fill the cobblestones of pedestrianized streets that no longer resemble the byways of Tenochtitlan, the Aztec capital, but history comes to life as you follow in their footsteps. Skipping through the centuries, you will see the foundation of the Aztec capital in 1325, the creation of the capital of New Spain, the independence of Mexico, the empire of Maximilian I, dictatorship, revolution, and earthquakes. This district bears witness to Mexico's history.

A degree of patience is needed in order to discover the charms of this bustling hub, where every street has its own specialty. Follow the Calle de Donceles and find yourself surrounded by photographic equipment stores, but not far away you will find booksellers and then stores packed with lamps and lightbulbs.

The traffic is chaotic these days. Such a huge population was never anticipated in these narrow streets, but somehow the area does not grind to a halt. It is noisy, of course, and disorganized, but once you get the hang of it and accept its rhythms, the city center begins to reveal its charms. You will find a sixteenth-century building transformed into a restaurant and a terrace looking out over the roof of the cathedral, along with a former religious school turned museum, and a potential surprise hidden behind every door.

Everything revolves around the Palacio de Bellas Artes, the fine arts museum. This is the cultural and artistic center of the city and home to a number of the country's most important frescoes (*murales*), bearing the signatures of Diego Rivera, José Clemente Orozco, and David Alfaro Siqueiros. Walk along Avenida Cinco de Mayo and you will reach Zócalo, Mexico's main square, where all the country's authorities are represented, dominated by an enormous Mexican flag: the sixteenth-century cathedral lies opposite the Palacio Nacional (the presidential palace) and this in turn adjoins the Suprema Corte de Justicia de la Nación (the Supreme Court).

THE ESSENTIALS

01

PALACIO DE BELLAS ARTES

Mexico's first opera house opened its doors in 1934 and features impressive frescoes by Rivera, Orozco, and Siqueiros.

02

CAFÉ DE TACUBA

This *cantina* has been dishing up classic Spanish cuisine since 1912, alongside a selection of *moles* (a sort of curry or sauce) in the purest Mexican tradition.

03

PASTELERÍA IDEAL

An iconic Mexican bakery founded in 1927 that sells all kinds of confectionery at great value prices.

04

COLEGIO DE SAN ILDEFONSO

Located just off Zócalo, what was once one of the biggest Jesuit colleges in the Americas is now a large museum, with works by a number of muralists.

05

MUSEO NACIONAL DE ARTE

The MUNAL houses a magnificent collection of Mexican art illustrating the history of the country from the pre-Columbian era to the turn of the twentieth century.

06

PALACIO DE CORREOS

A symbol of the modernism begun under Porfirio Díaz, this 1907 building is both a museum and the headquarters of the Mexican post office.

07

CASA DE LOS AZULEJOS

There is a restaurant and a souvenir store in this enormous bourgeois house, whose façade covered in handpainted tiles (*azulejos*) is immediately recognizable.

08

MUSEO MURAL DIEGO RIVERA

The must-see museum houses *Dream of a Sunday Afternoon in Alameda Park* (1947), Diego Rivera's famous fresco featuring about a hundred characters.

09

PLAZA DE SANTO DOMINGO

One of the capital's iconic squares, lined with buildings dating back to the eighteenth century, is packed with stands that specialize in printing counterfeit documents.

10

LA LAGUNILLA

The La Lagunilla district becomes a huge antiques market every Sunday that is popular with both locals and tourists.

11

BARRIO CHINO

This slightly contrived Chinatown near the Palacio de Bellas Artes is full of restaurants and stores for imported goods, and bears witness to Chinese immigration from the nineteenth century onwards.

12

CALLE DE DONCELES

You can visit the photography stores, bookstores, and antiquarians every day of the week on this street, which is very popular with students.

A confectionery seller of a certain age sets out his stall under the Zócalo arcades.

*Many of the buildings in the city center were built using volcanic rocks
from the still very active Popocatépetl.*

PLACE

CATEDRAL METROPOLITANA

SPANISH EVANGELISM

After the Spanish Conquest, Hernán Cortés ordered the construction of a church
on the site of the Templo Mayor, the largest Aztec place of worship.

FIRST CATHEDRAL

It was constructed in 1571 to replace America's very first cathedral, which had been completed in 1524.

SEISMIC ACTIVITY

The cathedral is constantly being repaired after suffering damage during the frequent earthquakes.

SPANISH ARCHITECTURE

A succession of different Spanish architects and engineers worked on its construction over the course of 250 years.

CATHOLICISM

Mexico is home to more Catholics than any other country in the world.

DOUBLE CATHEDRAL

A new cathedral was built on the site of the first in 1571.

OUR LADY OF GUADALUPE

An omnipresent figure in the conversion of Mexico.

DANGER OF COLLAPSE

Every year, the cathedral sinks another inch or so (2–3 cm) into the marshy ground on which it was built.

The Tlaquepaque taquería on Calle Isabel la Católica is renowned for its competitively priced
al pastor *(marinated pork) and* cabeza *(braised beef head/cheek) tacos.*

*The stores in the city center are arranged by specialty and by street and sell lamps,
children's games, old books, domestic appliances, etc.*

DEEP DIVE

MURALS AND MURALISTS

Muralism was a Mexican artistic movement promoted at the turn of the twentieth century by José Vasconcelos, the Minister of Education of the time. The idea was to create a link between the people and the history of the country by encouraging social awareness through immense historical frescoes painted on the walls of government buildings.

The frescoes invariably feature social criticism of the inequalities inherited from Porfirio Díaz's despotic regime. The topics addressed by the movement's main artists (Diego Rivera, Alfaro Siqueiros, and José Clemente Orozco) include indigenous and workers' rights, equality of opportunity, and criticism of capitalism, mass consumption, wars, and sacrifices.

The muralists aimed to transform painted space into an educational environment, documenting the historical events that had shaped their country in immense frescoes such as *New Democracy* (1944) by Siqueiros and Rivera's *Man at the Crossroads* (1934), both of which are to be found in the Palacio de Bellas Artes.

Rivera and Siqueiros were not natural political bedfellows; the former was a friend of Leon Trotsky, who visited him at his home in the district of Coyoacán, while the latter was a critic of the Communist system, but both militated for mass education and free public schools, and championed the teaching the pre- and post-colonial history of Mexico. Knowing that the most disadvantaged Mexicans were also illiterate, they made art in order to teach through images.

The Museo Diego Rivera lying opposite Alameda Central, a public park in the city center, is also home to one of the painter's most iconic works and the greatest tribute by an artist to his country; *Dream of a Sunday Afternoon in Alameda Park* is a fresco more than 50ft (15m) in length, telling 400 years of Mexican history and depicting more than a hundred iconic figures, including Rivera himself, Frida Kahlo, Hernán Cortés, Emiliano Zapata, and Posada's Catrina character.

José Clemente Orozco is known as the "Mexican Goya." His violent frescoes address the conditions of indigenous people and pre-Columbian civilizations, and all of his works are informed by biting social and political criticism. *The Trench*, which adorns the walls of the Antiguo Colegio de San Ildefonso in the city center, tells the story of the Mexican revolution through the death and sacrifice of workers and farmers.

LA CATRINA

In the middle stands La Catrina, a character created by José Guadalupe Posada, who holds the hands of her creator as a child.

FRIDA KAHLO

The artist, who was married to Diego Rivera, is depicted standing behind her husband. She rests one hand on his shoulder and in the other holds a ying and yang symbol.

DIEGO RIVERA

Diego Rivera is depicted as a child in the middle of the fresco, with a frog and a snake climbing out of his pockets.

PORFIRIO DÍAZ

José de la Cruz Porfirio Díaz Mori, general and politician, held the presidency of the Republic from 1876 until 1911.

EMILIANO ZAPATA

Iconic Mexican revolutionary who commanded the Liberation Army of the South from 1911.

HERNÁN CORTÉS

The Spanish conquistador, who was the first governor of New Spain, is depicted on the far left of the fresco.

A MONUMENTAL FRESCO

Dream of a Sunday Afternoon in Alameda Park (1947) is a fresco by Diego Rivera featuring more than a hundred figures that depict four centuries of Mexican history.

ABOVE

*The architecture of some of the buildings in the city center
reveals a fascination for European styles.*

OPPOSITE

*The Neoclassical touches of the Palacio de Bellas Artes façade
contrast with its Art deco interior.*

Mexico City is a megacity of more than 9 million inhabitants spread over 573 square miles (1,485km²).

PORTRAIT

COLECTIVO AMASIJO
A COMMITTED
FEMINIST CANTEEN

A very special welcome awaits at a venue in the historic center of Mexico City where both the ovens and the flame of ancestral knowledge are kept alight.

The Amasijo collective arose from a feminist cooking project bringing together women of various ages and professions who shared a common passion. The project began in 2016 and its leaders include Aureliana and Roselia Paz (two chefs from Veracruz), the economist Martina Manterola, and Carmen Serra, a cultural curator and graduate in Latin American literature.

The collective was born from a desire to care for, conserve, and celebrate local cooking. It facilitates and encourages an active exploration of the origins and diversity of dishes by deprivileging expertise and concentrating on learning by doing. Members listen to the stories of women who are close to the land while cooking together, to share, learn, and create connections.

The collective's culinary magic is cooked up in the heart of Seminario 12, a cultural center located opposite the cathedral. An enormous central worktop takes up almost all the space, and wicker baskets and terracotta pots contain all kinds of foodstuffs and spices: beans in every shape and size, oddly shaped tomatoes, multicolored corn kernels. It is a cabinet of curiosities from pre-Columbian Mexico.

People come here to learn, share, and listen. The collective offers a variety of initiatives that rethink food self-sufficiency by providing an alternative to supermarket fare and fast-food outlets, from workshops and conferences to private dinners, shamanic ceremonies, and a market that champions small producers and excellent produce.

This feminist collective organizes workshops, dinners, and a range of events exploring ideas of sovereignty and food autonomy.

CASA SEMINARIO

The oldest inhabited residence in Mexico City stands at 12, Calle Seminario. It now houses a hotel, stores, and a cooking workshop.

ABOVE

*The colorful façades contrast with the black asphalt and
volcanic rock of the streets and sidewalks.*

OPPOSITE

*Tacos and other street food specialties are available at
any time of the day or night.*

PORTRAIT

MOÍSES ESCUDERO
MANAGER OF LA ÓPERA, A HISTORIC AND TRADITIONAL *CANTINA*

La Ópera is not a traditional Mexican *cantina*. Nor is it a bar or restaurant, and it's certainly not a tourist trap, but instead it is a piece of history, a symbol, a legend, and a journey back in time to a Mexico that has almost disappeared.

Anyone will tell you that this is the *cantina* where you can see the traces left by a bullet fired into the ceiling by Pancho Villa. More than just a bullet, however, it was indeed a message. The Mexican revolutionary, a child of the people and defender of the poorest and most disadvantaged, intended to leave a reminder of his presence in this bastion of the Mexican aristocracy, the preserve of the politicians and intelligentsia of the Porfirio era.

Just walk through this door on the Avenida Cinco de Mayo, one of the city center's greatest avenues, and you will be taken on a journey through time. The décor includes woodcarvings with thousands of details, contemporary watercolors, and faded, blackened mirrors, with an almost complete lack of modern elements to suggest the contemporary period. A visit is worthwhile for the immense Art nouveau bar alone.

Sitting where figures as illustrious as Porfirio Díaz, Emiliano Zapata, Octavio Paz, Carlos Fuentes, Fernando Botero, and Gabriel García Márquez

once sat, and ordering what they ordered, feels like sharing a moment in history, or at least, a moment in their daily lives.

Cradling a *sangrita* (a kind of highly spiced tomato juice, the perfect accompaniment to a *caballito* of tequila and a house specialty), Moíses Escudero tells us of the day that Gabriel García Márquez, the renowned author of *One Hundred Years of Solitude*, refused to autograph a patron's napkin and went out to buy some of his own books to sign for him.

What makes Moíses Escudero particularly proud, however, is that this is a place where you can still enjoy certain traditional dishes that have otherwise almost vanished, such as *caracoles al chipotle* (snails in *chipotle* sauce) and *pulpo a la gallega* (Galician-style octopus), in a place brimming with history and life, where all ages can mingle and *trios de cuerdas* (string trios) have played the same tunes for decades. Tradition is not just followed here but respected.

The menu at one of the city's oldest restaurants has all the finest Galician specialties, including the famous *caracoles a la gallega*.

ANECDOTE

Revolutionaries, corrupt politicians, and writers of international renown have all been regulars at La Ópera.

ABOVE

Mexico's forty million dogs are proof that the country is pet friendly.

OPPOSITE

*Roofs are coated with thick layers of waterproof paint intended to provide
protection from the heavy rains that fall between June and October.*

ABOVE

*The streets teem with ice-cream sellers during the dry season
(spring and fall).*

OPPOSITE

*The Dulcería de Celaya has been selling sweet treats from the
state of Guanajuato since 1874.*

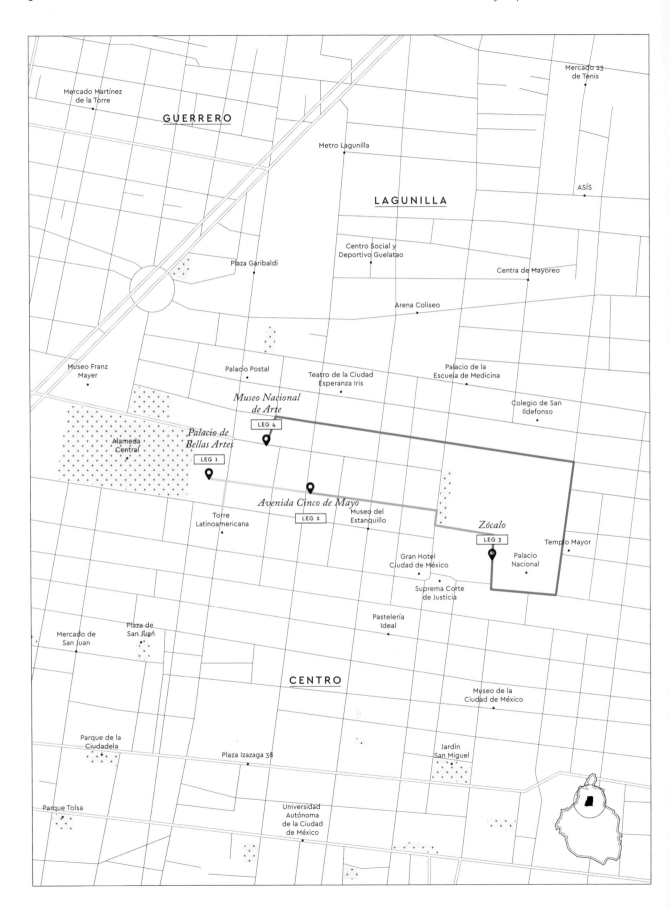

Mercado 23
de Tenis

Mercado Martínez
de la Torre

GUERRERO

Metro Lagunilla

ASÍS

LAGUNILLA

Centro Social y
Deportivo Guelatao

Plaza Garibaldi

Centra de Mayoreo

Arena Coliseo

Museo Franz
Mayer

Palacio Postal

Teatro de la Ciudad
Esperanza Iris

Palacio de la
Escuela de Medicina

*Museo Nacional
de Arte*

Colegio de San
Ildefonso

LEG 4

Alameda
Central

*Palacio de
Bellas Artes*

LEG 1

Torre
Latinoamericana

Avenida Cinco de Mayo

LEG 2

Museo del
Estanquillo

Zócalo

LEG 3

Templo Mayor

Gran Hotel
Ciudad de México

Palacio
Nacional

Suprema Corte
de Justicia

Pastelería
Ideal

Mercado de
San Juan

Plaza de
San Juan

CENTRO

Museo de la
Ciudad de México

Parque de la
Ciudadela

Plaza Izazaga 38

Jardín
San Miguel

Parque Tolsa

Universidad
Autónoma
de la Ciudad
de México

TRAVELING THROUGH TIME IN THE HEART OF THE HISTORIC CITY CENTER

Nearly two million Mexicans throng the streets of the world's largest historic city center every weekend.

LEG 1: BELLAS ARTES, A REAL GEM

The gradated coloration of its roof, from yellow to reddish orange, has made it one of the most iconic buildings in Mexico City, and a climb to the top of the Torre Latinoamericana delivers a panoramic view across the entire city, with the bonus of a bird's-eye view of one of the most beautiful rooftops in the country. As majestic as the exterior of the Palacio de Bellas Artes may be, it is the interior that will take your breath away, with its marble staircases, period chandeliers, and incredibly delicate wrought iron.

Most compelling, however, are the walls covered with masterpiece frescoes by Orozco, Rivera, and Siqueiros. These impressive revolutionary works shock and surprise in equal measure in this bastion of Mexican art.

LEG 2: FROM ALAMEDA TO ZÓCALO

More than two million Mexicans take to the pedestrianized streets of the city center every weekend to enjoy a family breakfast, do some shopping, take a stroll, or relive a little of the history of their country. Leaving Alameda Central (an immense square dotted with fountains in the shade of century-old trees), take either Avenida Cinco de Mayo (the date of the Mexican victory against the French at the Battle of Puebla in 1862) or Avenida Francisco Madero to reach Zócalo, the religious, judicial, and historical heart of Mexico City.

LEG 3: ZÓCALO

An immense Mexican flag hangs over this vast square. To the north is the imposing bulk of the Metropolitan Cathedral, built in 1571 by the Spanish on the still-smoldering ruins of the Templo Mayor Aztec shrine, of which only traces remain. The Palacio Nacional on the southern side is the official residence of the president of the republic, while the Suprema Corte de Justicia in the southwest corner makes up the third of this mighty triumvirate.

LEG 4: CULTURE, TRADITION, AND HAGGLING

The city center boasts a staggering wealth of culture, both high and low. The Museo Nacional de Arte is worth a visit, if only for its Neoclassical architecture. Just around the corner, the Palacio Postal, covered in gilt detailing, is considered one of the most beautiful buildings in the country (as indeed are the Gran Hotel Ciudad de México and the Sanborns de los Azulejos opposite). Each one embodies an era, a culture, and a tradition that is still vibrant. The Calle de Donceles, farther to the north, never ceases to amaze; over a mile long (2 km), it is crammed with camera stores, antiquarian booksellers, and outlets selling domestic appliances, lamps, and school supplies. The haggling is intense, the pace frenetic, and the crowds limitless, and the only option for escaping the relentless throng is either to take refuge in the Antiguo Colegio de San Ildefonso, a former monastery that has been turned into a museum, or on one of the city center's many rooftops from where you can view this anthill from a new angle.

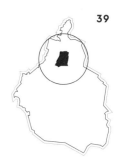

BETWEEN BOURGEOISIE AND REVOLUTION

ROMA
NORTE AND SUR

Roma, a bustling, creative, and festive area famous for its food,
tree-lined squares, and Art deco buildings, has been immortalized
on the silver screen in Alfonso Cuarón's film of the same name.

P. 38

The Edificio Anáhuac at 109, Calle Querétaro is an
Art deco masterpiece.

OPPOSITE

Water supply issues mean that water tankers crisscross the city.

At the end of the nineteenth century, Porfirio Díaz resolved to build a district that would rival any European or North American city, and Roma certainly attracts the country's elite. Art nouveau and Art deco buildings sprang up like mushrooms, and the boom in the district's growth remained unchecked, even by the Mexican revolution. "Porfirio's orphan" would eventually even become the home of some of the revolutionaries themselves, once the harshest critics of the bourgeoisie and the excesses of the previous regime.

The area suffered major damage in the earthquake that rocked Mexico City in 1985, leaving scars that are visible to this day, but some 1,500 listed buildings still grace the streets of a district that was once the city's darling. It has rebuilt itself gradually, aided by migrants from every corner of Latin America. The Colombian district along Avenida Medellín beats to the rhythms of its eponymous market and new flavors can be discovered in the Venezuelan district a little farther on, where *tortillas* become *arepas* and the colorful walls celebrate the unity of all Latinos.

The squares of Río de Janeiro and Luis Cabrera lie opposite one another in the heart of Roma Norte, separated only by the Avenida Álvaro Obregón. You will soon be aware that nothing stands still here; modern and traditional rub shoulders and street food competes with the finest restaurants. Dancers of all ages fill the *cantinas* while the clandestine nightclubs attract a young crowd until the early hours.

Roma Norte wants to be a bustling party zone, but the charm of Roma Sur is more discreet and authentic. Whole generations in this residential area have witnessed the gentrification of one of the most central and attractive corners of the city and yet the locals have survived these developments and held their ground; knife-sharpeners still go door to door, water and gas deliverymen announce their presence with ear-splitting yells, and the small stores look as if they have been frozen in time in a Mexico City of the past.

Roma is an urban museum and a relic of the convoluted history of modern-day Mexico. This multifaceted, multicultural district is full of contradictions and still attracts increasing numbers of emigrants and tourists every year.

THE ESSENTIALS

FUENTE DE CIBELES

This copy of the famous Fountain of Cybele in Madrid celebrates the friendship
that has existed between the Spanish and Mexican communities since
the end of the twentieth century.

14

CINE TONALÁ

A renowned art-house movie theater with a tiny screening room of about fifty seats.

15

CASA BOSQUES

This art bookstore tucked away upstairs in a historic house on Calle Córdoba is one of the most avant-garde in the country.

16

MERCADO MEDELLÍN

This local market is a culinary and gastronomic melting pot for the whole of Latin America and is famous for its specialties from Yucatán, Tabasco, Cuba, and Colombia.

17

EL PARIÁN

This arcade lined with restaurants and small stores opened at the turn of the twentieth century and was renovated in 2022.

18

PLAZA RÍO DE JANEIRO

This square in the heart of Roma was completed in 1903 and is now a haven of tranquility loved by locals for its cool air and lush vegetation.

19

ORINOCO

A taco chain from Monterrey known for its *chicharrón* (crispy pork skin) tacos.

ABOVE

*Following in the footsteps of the great muralists, Mexican artists
are often invited to reinvent the streets.*

OPPOSITE

*The creativity of residents is demonstrated in the radiant colors
of these façades.*

PLACE

MERCADO DE MEDELLÍN

Lying between Medellín and Monterrey Avenues in Roma district, Mercado Medellín is a cultural and culinary crossroads for the whole of Latin America.

Known for its specialties from Yucatán, Tabasco, Cuba, and Colombia, Mercado Medellín is a riot of stalls displaying vegetables and colorful and sweet fruit, many of which you can be forgiven for not recognizing since they are unique to South America. From cassava root to tapioca, dragon fruit to *lulo* (a small, orange fruit from the Andean countries also known as *naranjilla*), there is something to suit every occasion and taste.

You can't go wrong if you decide to eat out locally. Check out the many stands, each one different from the last; improvised kitchens compete creatively to dish up every kind of exotic cuisine, from *cochinita pibil* (pork marinated in orange juice and annatto, a traditional Mayan spice) straight from the Yucatán peninsula, to Venezuelan *arepas* and *cachapas* (corn pancakes filled with cheese), *bandeja paisa* (a traditional Colombian dish made up of rice, ground beef, chorizo, an egg, and various sauces), and a thousand other Latin specialties that you need to try. This market is a microcosm of the whole country. A cosmopolitan and welcoming place, it is a mirror of the cultural and culinary capital of Latin America as a whole. You will even find coca leaves from Bolivia and Inca Kola (a traditional Peruvian soda).

Many people visit the market to eat, but locals also like to stock up on flowers at the stalls laden with magnificent blooms with exquisite colors and exotic scents. Turn a corner and you will discover someone selling *peltre*, enameled metal pans that are very popular in Latin America, and not far away a locksmith, a gift wrap seller, a *piñata*-maker, an enormous candy stall, or a hardware store. Time stands still as local life takes over in a district that, despite gentrification and the exponential growth of the city, seems to have remained frozen in the 1970s.

Lose yourself in the narrow alleyways of the market, crammed with shoppers, to really appreciate all it has to offer. Embark on this sensual adventure without preconceptions or fear of the unknown. Take your time, stop regularly and ask questions, and uncover the secrets of one of the most colorful markets in Mexico City.

Colombian fruit, Cuban snacks, Chilean food…
a stroll through the Mercado Medellín is like a
journey across Latin America.

A CULTURAL CROSSROADS

Colombian, Venezuelan, and Cuban communities
have gradually grown up around the market,
sharing their cultures and traditions.

ABOVE

*Flowers, trees, and plants take over the sidewalks,
sometimes making life complicated for pedestrians.*

OPPOSITE

*The best way to explore the peace and quiet of the
area's shady streets is on foot.*

Small traders and specialist artisans are standing up to the big brands with high-quality service at low prices.

A completely renovated Volkswagen combi van outside a boutique hotel on Calle San Luis Potosi.

Visit the stalls on the corner of Avenidas Insurgentes Sur and Álvaro Obregón for a unique and truly local experience at a great price.

DEEP DIVE

ANTOJITOS MEXICANOS

IN THE COUNTRY OF CORN, STREET FOOD IS KING

What do *empanadas, sopes, quesadillas, flautas, tlacoyos, enchiladas, tamales, chalupas,* and *chilaquiles* all have in common?
Corn, obviously.

Street food in Mexico City is fascinating for foodies and linguists. With all their flavors and traditions, *antojitos* ("little cravings" or "small tasty bites," ie appetizers) are a culinary universe that is as delicious as it is infinite. The average person in the street would struggle to spot the difference between a *sope* and a *memela*, however, largely because there is often none at all, despite the difference in terminology.

Every version has its unique characteristics: a *tortilla* with meat is a taco, but a *tortilla* topped with meat and cheese is a *quesadilla*. A slightly thicker *tortilla* is known as a *sope*. Fry a *tortilla* and it becomes a *panucho*. Roll it before you fry it, and you have a delicious *flauta*. You will need time, patience, a good memory, and a dash of courage to work through every Mexican *antojito*; there are more than 150 versions, and even Mexicans themselves will disagree about what to call their culinary miracles.

Crossing borders and traveling through time, some of these dishes have been inherited from pre-Columbian civilizations: a *tamal*, from the Nahuatl word *tamalli* (wrapped), is a sheet of nixtamalized (cooked in lime water) cornflour dough that is steamed and wrapped in a corn husk or banana leaf, depending on the region. You will see *tamales* with chicken or pork, or filled with *salsa verde*, red beans, or even sweet beans, and neon pink in color. The capital is also renowned for one of its greatest culinary inventions, *guajolota*, which is essentially a *tamal* eaten as a sandwich; a handful of pesos will get you a 1,000-calorie snack.

Mexico City street food has a certain reputation for being heavy, oily, fatty, and not particularly good for you, but you will experience unique flavors and textures, such as *huitlacoche*, a mushroom that grows on certain ears of corn and is known as "Mexican truffle."

The bravest adventurer may discover that there is a gastric price to pay for such good value delights, but every taste is catered for and nothing is bad. Pay close attention to your choice of *salsa*, however; every self-respecting *antojito* comes accompanied by several *salsas* that are as key to the experience as they are fiery and, above all, never trust a Mexican who tries to tell you the sauce is "not hot". It's a lie!

ANTOJITOS AND MASA DE MAÍZ

TAMAL

Filled corn dough, wrapped in a
corn husk and steamed.

TLACOYOS

A thick corn *tortilla* topped with
black beans and other ingredients.

TACOS

A corn *tortilla* with various toppings,
onion, and cilantro.

PANUCHOS

A fried corn *tortilla* topped
with black beans.

QUESADILLAS

A wheat or corn *tortilla*
filled with cheese.

ELOTES

A cooked corn cob with mayonnaise,
lemon juice, and chili powder.

ESQUITE

Grilled sweetcorn, mayonnaise,
lemon juice, and chili powder.

GORDITAS

A thick corn *tortilla* that is fried and served
with a range of ingredients.

ENCHILADAS

A filled corn *tortilla* that is rolled and
doused in sauce.

MASA DE MAÍZ

Masa de maíz is cornmeal that has been worked to form
a pliable dough, and is mainly used in making various *antojitos*
(*enchiladas*, *tamales*, tacos).

ARTS AND CRAFTS

LA LAGUNA DOCTORES

A BASTION OF CONTEMPORARY ART

A young community of artists and entrepreneurs are reinventing cohabitation in this former textile factory.

ARTISTS' WORKSHOPS

These condos host artists from around the globe all year round.

MINI-BAR

A bar frequented by both passersby and workers is located upstairs in a block made entirely of concrete.

YOUNG ENTREPRENEURS

Creators, artists, and inventors share airy, open-plan workspaces.

CERAMICS

Ceramicists show their work and organize workshops to teach their skills.

ARTS AND CRAFTS

Tea importers, design studios, art bookstores, La Laguna is full of artsy folk.

JOINERY

La Metropolitana creates unique furniture from high-quality timber.

COMMUNITY

Hand-picked members of the community share their creations in a unique space.

ABOVE

*In earthquake zones, it is not uncommon to see buildings with cracks
that have been repaired with whatever is to hand.*

OPPOSITE

*Enormous water tanks are kept on rooftops (known as azoteas)
that are also used as little private terraces.*

ABOVE

The owner of a grocery store keeps a careful eye on his
slot machines on Avenida Cuauhtémoc.

OPPOSITE

Loncherías, *whose name is derived from the word "lunch,"*
serve midday meals and sandwiches at affordable prices.

ELENA REYGADAS

REDEFINING MEXICAN "BREAD"

Elena Reygadas's resumé is as impressive as the simplicity
with which Latin America's greatest prize-winning chef
welcomes us on the terrace of her bakery Panadería Rosetta.

The restaurant at Rosetta has been attracting gourmets from all over the world since 2010. It serves Italian-influenced, international cuisine that has never forgotten its Mexican roots.

Elena Reygadas is an excellent cook for whom sharing is non-negotiable. When she opened her first restaurant, she started placing a loaf of bread (baked on-site) on the tables, accompanied by a little olive oil. The idea, she says, was to "invite diners to break bread together, to break the ice, to get to know one another – to share."

She tells us how when she started baking bread for her restaurant over a decade ago, she would get calls from locals and restaurant owners to ask if the batch was ready yet. It was difficult to get European-style bread in Mexico City in 2010, and this is how the eponymous bakery just around the corner from the restaurant came about.

Local residents soon started turning up to enjoy a coffee and read the newspaper before leaving with a *concha* (a round, spongy, often vanilla-flavored pastry shaped like a shell). Created by chance, the bar was to become her trademark.

Elena tells of the loving relationship that unites Mexicans with *pan*. It is important to know that in Mexico City bread is predominantly *dulce* (gentle, in the sense of sweet) and for special occasions. To celebrate the arrival of the Three Wise Men, people share some *rosca* (crown), and on All Saints' Day they eat *pan de muerto* ("bread of the dead"). Bread also features in idioms; you should have a *bolillo para el susto* ("a little loaf for a great fear") or nibble on pastries to recover from a romantic break-up, as with *con pan las penas son menos* ("sorrows are less with bread").

We then discuss the huge success enjoyed by *rol de guayaba* (guava roll), the cult pastry she created because she wished to make a Mexican bread with local flavors that paid tribute to the country's incredible culinary wealth. This must-have has become a classic, up there with *pan de pulque* (a loaf made with a traditional pre-Columbian drink based on maguey agave), *pan de ceniza* (ash bread), and *envuelto de estragón* (tarragon roll), her favorite.

Croissants and chocolate treats share space with local creations celebrating Mexican flavors, such as the iconic *rol de guayaba* (guava roll).

A MEETING PLACE

Before cementing her place as a local figure, Elena would stand behind her large bar to receive the customers who would mingle in her bakery.

ABOVE

*Many signwriters in Mexico City decorate display windows
and storefronts by hand.*

OPPOSITE

*The terrace of a cheap and cheerful restaurant in Romita district,
with plastic floral tablecloths and colorful stools.*

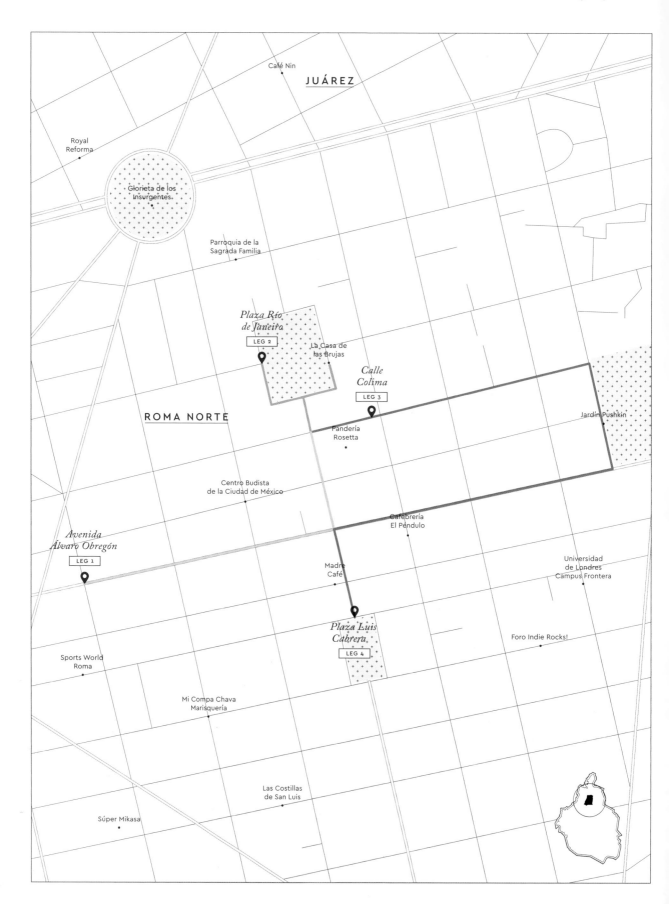

Café Nin

JUÁREZ

Royal
Reforma

Glorieta de los
Insurgentes

Parroquia de la
Sagrada Familia

*Plaza Río
de Janeiro*
LEG 2

La Casa de
las Brujas

*Calle
Colima*
LEG 3

ROMA NORTE

Jardín Pushkin

Panadería
Rosetta

Centro Budista
de la Ciudad de México

Cafebrería
El Péndulo

*Avenida
Álvaro Obregón*
LEG 1

Madre
Café

Universidad
de Londres
Campus Frontera

*Plaza Luis
Cabrera*
LEG 4

Foro Indie Rocks!

Sports World
Roma

Mi Compa Chava
Marisquería

Las Costillas
de San Luis

Súper Mikasa

MEXICO CITY: TRENDY AND OUT THERE

Some of the best restaurants, the coolest bars, and the craziest concept stores in the country are clustered around Avenida Álvaro Obregón, Calle Colima, Plaza Río de Janeiro, and Plaza Luis Cabrera. It is the place to eat at, go out to, and be seen.

LEG 1: A STROLL ALONG ÁLVARO OBREGÓN

The Avenida Álvaro Obregón is one of the few Mexican thoroughfares to have a central reservation, making it ideal for a Sunday stroll and a perfect starting-point for exploring the district. It is home to the headquarters of the Communist party, along with antiques stores, chic restaurants, and street food stalls. Feast your eyes and indulge all your other senses as you stroll down the boulevard, where the buildings (from the last century) are reminiscent of Haussmann's finest work in Paris.

LEG 2: WAVES OF FLAVORS ON CALLE COLIMA

Running parallel to the impressive Avenida Álvaro Obregón, Calle Colima is more discreet, more secluded, and even more shaded, and is considered one of the city's most beautiful streets. It has become an icon of gentrification and you will find the best restaurants in its Porfirio-era villas, including chef Elena Reygadas's Rosetta. Fashionable start-ups and trendy companies have set up shop here and even the museums aspire to be cool and hip, such as the Museo del Objeto, which exhibits more than 140,000 household items. Visit for the small stores selling vintage clothes, jewelry, and craft pottery made from Oaxaca's *barro negro* ("black earth").

LEG 3: PLAZA RÍO DE JANEIRO

Lying halfway between Avenida de los Insurgentes and Jardín Pushkin, Plaza Río de Janeiro boasts some of the most impressive buildings in the area. At number 56 is the Casa de las Brujas ("witches' house") with its Victorian façade, black spire (shaped like a pointy hat, hence the name), and Art deco interior, but the frenzy of European influences does not stop there; turn your head slightly to see a bronze replica of Michaelangelo's *David*, installed in 1976. The calm and shade of the surrounding streets has been quickly swamped by trendy bars and restaurants frequented by fine diners and gastronomes at all hours of the day and night.

LEG 4: PLAZA LUIS CABRERA

Plaza Luis Cabrera on the other side of the avenue refuses to be outdone, however, and caters for every taste, from Texan barbecue to a Parisian brew bar with craft beers. The central fountain is an ideal place to cool off in the shade of its lime trees, as Mexico City's heat and elevation make longer walks exhausting.

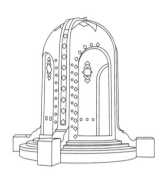

A BOHEMIAN CENTER OF COSMOPOLITAN CHIC

CONDESA

Come to Ciudad de México and you may well find
Condesa both surprising and challenging, but it won't leave you indifferent.
The area was created at the turn of the twenty-first century and has
attracted artists, bohemians, and intellectuals from around the world.
It has become a place where life is good.

P. 6 8

An example of the area's bohemian chic style on the corner of
Calle Cuernavaca and Calle Alfonso Reyes; bespoke ironwork, mosaic detailing,
decorated façades, and the ever-present shade from the trees.

OPPOSITE

Carts and stalls sell fresh fruit, often accompanied by salt,
lemon juice, and Chamoy sauce.

This area has evolved on land that once belonged to the Santa María del Arenal hacienda acquired by the Countess of Miravalle in the eighteenth century, hence the name. This colorful character built a racecourse outside her residence (which now houses the Russian embassy), and its curves and straights eventually became Avenida Ámsterdam, one of the city's most popular and creative avenues. It forms a loop around which architects have designed several masterpieces for the area, from the iconic Edificio Condesa (1911) to the equally prestigious Casa Mondrian.

In the center of this loop lies Parque México, a recreational area to which *Chilangos* (as Mexico City residents are known) come in the evening and on weekends to enjoy leisure activities that range from boxing classes to yoga training, cheerleading to salsa. There are dogs everywhere; Mexico City is one of the most pet-friendly towns in the world. The sheer number of endemic trees and plants is breathtaking in itself. It is an urban jungle, splendid and chaotic, surrounded by solid-looking buildings from the last century proudly displaying their names (Edificio Teresa, Edificio San Martín, etc), relics of the area's golden age in the 1930s and 1940s.

Unfortunately, the earthquake of September 1985 destroyed large parts of the area, and it was not until the 2000s that Condesa rose from the ashes, when Mexico City was suddenly fashionable. Artists like Gabriel Orozco began shining a spotlight on a city with a reputation for being chaotic and dangerous, and this sudden international fame drew tourists, emigrants, and investors, helping the area to rediscover its former glory.

Don't be surprised to hear French, English, Russian, or German spoken on the street; expatriates looking for space and creativity have flocked to this new urban Eldorado, opening restaurants, bars, terraces, and bookstores, and preserving the charm of the old even as they construct the Mexico City of tomorrow.

THE ESSENTIALS

20

HOTEL CONDESA DF

This hotel on the corner of Avenida Veracruz and Avenida Guadalajara
near Parque España pays homage to Mexican design and cuisine.

21

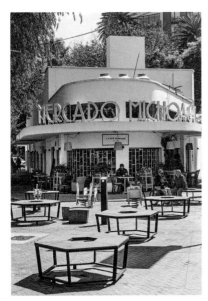

MOLINO EL PUJOL

The renowned chef Enrique Olvera uses local produce in his high-end *tortillería*.

22

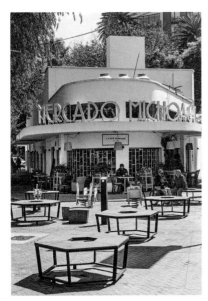

MERCADO MICHOACÁN

You will find everything in the local covered market, from fresh fruits and seasonal vegetables to traditional Mexican cooking and world cuisine, with flowers for the table at bargain prices.

23

LA INCREÍBLE

Lovers of beautiful books and witty sayings gather at La Increíble to share a coffee and discuss the books they are reading.

24

FONDO DE CULTURA ECONÓMICA

The FCE was founded in 1934 and is now Mexico's largest publishing house; it often hosts literary events such as book signings.

25

PLAZA POPOCATÉPETL

Locals consider the small fountain on Plaza Popocatépetl to be the very heart of the area.

26

LA ESQUINA DEL CHILAQUIL

Customers wait in their dozens in this culinary institution for a chance to devour a *torta de chilaquiles*, a spicy and calorific sandwich.

ABOVE

*Residents of the capital frequent their favorite taquería at all hours;
the most authentic spots have terraces where you can eat standing
at the counter or sitting on a stool.*

OPPOSITE

*Vegetation (banana trees, cactuses) is king along Avenida Ámsterdam,
although plants often break up the sidewalks.*

ABOVE

*The Distrito Federal officially became the Ciudad de México in 2014.
The city chose the color pink to mark this change,
which now decorates the capital's taxis.*

OPPOSITE

*The hule (rubber tree) thrives in Mexico City and its enormous roots
often lift roads and sidewalks.*

*The Mexican capital is infamous for the parlous state of its streets,
and potholes are legion.*

*With 518 endemic species of cactus, Mexico is undoubtedly the
country of succulents. Just be careful where you put your fingers!*

JESÚS SALAS TORNÉS

NO MENU, BUT PLENTY OF CREATIVITY

Expendio de Maíz Sin Nombre is not a traditional restaurant,
but rather a culinary, cultural, social, architectural,
and accountable experience.

Hailing from Guerrero, Jesús Salas Tornés is the scion of a farming family. As chef and owner of Expendio (a term denoting a small grocery store that sells essentials), he has created a place where his passion for sharing and rural cuisine can be expressed.

Having grown up in the countryside, he is reinterpreting rural Mexican cuisine with pride and skill. His dishes are mainly vegetarian as a reminder that meat is a luxury and showcase exceptional produce sourced from small-scale producers. The ingredients he works with are hand selected and all impeccably traceable back to the farm.

The cooks at Expendio work around a central fire that never goes out. This tiny space was created to order by the French architect Ludwig Godefroy using local stone. Terracotta plates (many of which are chipped) and basalt *molcajetes* (Mesoamerican mortars and pestles) lie piled up beside woven baskets straight out of Oaxaca or Veracruz, bananas hang on a hook awaiting use, and you can hardly move for enormous glass jars of mezcal. This is an Ali Baba's cave unlike any other kitchen, and for a good reason; Jesús is unlike any other cook.

There is no menu at Expendio. It reinvents itself every single day according to the inspiration of the cooks and whatever has arrived in the kitchen. Nothing is written down so there is nothing to insist on ordering, and patrons know the rules of the game; you can never be sure what you are going to get. The approach seems to work, however, as is clear from the almost two-hour wait in line that can be expected by those who happen to turn up a bit late.

And yet Jesús hasn't really invented anything; he is just cooking good produce with simplicity, and corn is the essential ingredient at the heart of his project; he sources his supplies from exceptional producers cultivating the *cacahuazintle* variety at elevations above 11,155 ft (3,400 m) and nixtamalizes what he needs every night.

In a country of *tortillas* and agri-food, Jesús is swimming against the tide. He is educating palates and creating new ways of living from farming. He is fighting for a reassessment of corn and Mexican expertise, shining a spotlight on the work of cooks and creating in his own image a possible future for the restaurant trade: a kind of functional chaos, creative, improvised, and bursting with flavor.

NO MENU

The chef improvises with whatever is fresh in each day, to the delight of his customers.

RESPECTING THE PRODUCE

Local corn, *tortillas* cooked directly on the *comal*, heirloom tomatoes, and exceptional produce; simplicity and excellence are the order of the day.

ABOVE

Small buses have been providing reliable routes across the city since the 1960s.
Dubbed peseros, *the nickname has survived to this day.*

OPPOSITE

Microbuses cross Mexico City according to their own rules
and at top speed! They are often on time, however.

P. 84-5

Bars and restaurants on Avenida Tamaulipas attract a mixture of
young people and tourists in the evenings.

HISTORY

THE CRAZY HISTORY
OF EMPEROR MAXIMILIAN

The political history of Mexico is full of ambitions, changes, and constant convolutions; the brief reign of the emperor Maximilian is a perfect example of this.

After three centuries of Spanish occupation, the people of Mexico rose up when the priest Miguel Hidalgo issued a call to arms from his parish in Dolores during the night of September 15, 1810. History has recorded this moment as *el Grito de Dolores* ("Cry of Dolores") and eleven years of war were to follow, culminating in the independence of Mexico, declared on September 27, 1821. In July 1822, Agustín de Iturbide, the leader of the independence movement, was crowned emperor of Mexico, but his reign lasted only seven months; dozens of politicians then led the country until the French intervened with a military invasion.

In 1862, Benito Juárez, the president of the republic, had decided to suspend repayment of the country's foreign debt and its creditors (Spain, England, and Napoleon III's France) resolved to send troops to Veracruz. When the French landed in Mexico the following year, Juárez sought refuge in the north of the country where he organized guerilla resistance. Napoleon III, who wished to create a Latin empire in America, asked Marshal Forey to bring together thirty-five prominent Mexicans as an assembly with a view to adopting the monarchical system and offering the imperial crown to Archduke Maximilian of Austria, a Habsburg aristocrat.

Maximilian accepted the throne on April 10, 1864, installing himself (along with his wife, Charlotte) in Chapultepec castle in Mexico a month later. He undertook a top-to-bottom restructuring of the country, guaranteeing freedom of the press, reopening the university, nationalizing the assets of the clergy, instituting a civil register, promulgating divorce legislation, and drafting the first Mexican labor laws.

The liberal choices made by the young emperor did not please his European backers, however, and, under pressure from Prussia, they withdrew their economic and military support. The tide began to turn as General Porfirio Díaz's troops besieged Mexico City and the emperor fled to Querétaro.

Juárez took Querétaro in 1867, capturing Maximilian and sentencing him to death. Neither correspondence from Victor Hugo nor intervention by Charlotte was enough to save the unfortunate prisoner and he was executed by firing squad, along with his generals, on the Cerro de las Campanas (Hill of Bells). Legend has it that his last words were "poor Charlotte!"

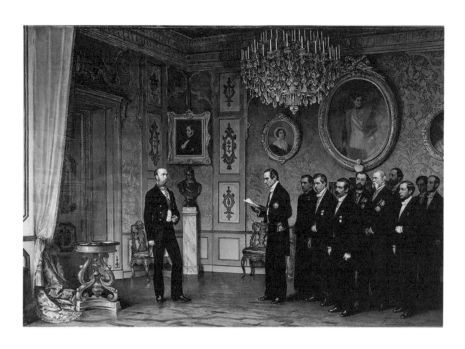

*Just after becoming ruler of the country, Emperor Maximilian received
an assembly of thirty-five dignitaries in Chapultepec castle.*

*Manet painted the execution of Emperor Maximilian, who was shot on
June 19, 1867, on the Cerro de las Campanas in the state of Querétaro.*

Rótulos *(hand-painted signs) showcase Mexican creativity and skill.*

*Paradise for architects: the earthquakes that rock the capital destroy the old
and give birth to the modern.*

*This famous family locksmith's has been
based in the area since 1931.*

*Art deco style was fashionable with the capital's rich property
owners halfway through the twentieth century.*

NATURE

PARQUE
MÉXICO

CHURROS

Endless snack options are on offer in the park,
from *churros* to corn on the cob slathered in mayonnaise.

MULTI-ACTIVITY

There's room for everything, from skateboarding to boxing lessons.

URBAN OASIS

The park opened in 1921 and has become one of the area's top attractions.

ARCHITECTURE

Every preference is catered for, from Art deco and Art nouveau to contemporary architecture.

BOUGAINVILLEA

Vegetation thrives in the humid climate of spring.

A DOGGY PARADISE

Pet friendly; our four-legged friends have an easy life here.

FORO LINDBERGH

The park forum is a popular meeting place.

ADOPTION

Dozens of dogs are put up for adoption every weekend.

OPEN-AIR LESSONS

Lessons are available in every discipline, from salsa to pickleball.

ABOVE

*Avenida México, which runs along the west side of Parque México,
is an ideal starting point for exploring on foot.*

OPPOSITE

*The park is an urban jungle and a rendezvous for dog owners,
locals, and curious tourists.*

DEEP DIVE

TACOS

MEXICO'S GIFT TO THE WHOLE WORLD

Controversy and disagreement are baked into this
Mexican specialty that has become fashionable to eat on the go,
in the street, or in the hip restaurants.

There seems to be no consensus on where or how the most popular and famous Mexican dish was created, or indeed who was responsible. Some people attribute it to northern miners, who used to wrap their lunch in corn *tortillas* to protect it and keep the meat and vegetables warm, just as they used sheets of paper to wrap up the gunpowder used in the mines. Others, including the Franciscan missionary Bernardino de Sahagún, have suggested that the word *taco* comes from the Nahuatl *tlahco* (half of a thing). But what is a taco, if not a *tortilla* filled with your choice of meat, vegetables, rice, or sauce? Other correlations with Nahuatl leave little doubt about the obvious connection between taco and food; the word *tlaquliztli* means the action of eating or the meal itself, while *tlaqualli* refers both to a particular dish and to anything eaten in general, while *quauhtlaqualli* is the name given to large *tortillas* of white corn that are reserved for kings.

If the origins of the dish remain obscure, there is complete agreement that a taco is a *tortilla* (made of corn, wheat, or even nopal [prickly pear], or a lettuce leaf), with a filling of your choice, topped with sauce, lemon, onions, and cilantro. It is simple and cheap food that can be eaten with one's hands, and there is a taco for every preference and budget.

Mexican inventiveness has done the rest; there are more than sixty different taco types in Mexico City alone. Are you tempted by a taco with beef scraps, pork tripe, chicken feet, or sheep stomach? If you're in the mood for something a bit more mainstream, go for a taco *al pastor*, made with pork marinated in annatto, skewered like a kabob, and served with delicate pieces of pineapple. To add a Mayan touch, choose a *taco de cochinita pibil* (pork cooked in a hole in the ground), marinated in a mix of spices and orange juice and topped with red onions.

A WORLD OF TACOS

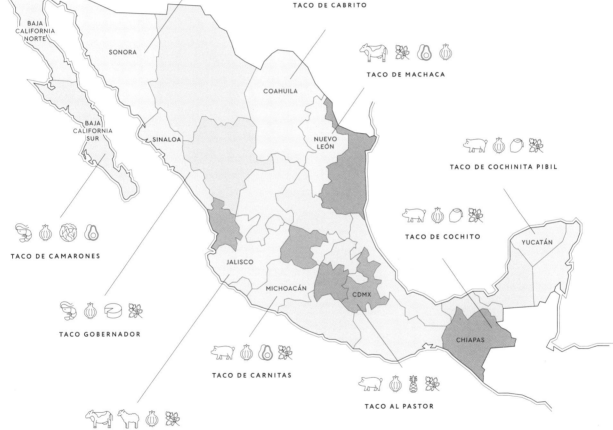

EVERY STATE HAS ITS OWN SPECIALTY

A *tortilla* made of corn or wheat, a filling that often features meat,
some vegetables, some chili, a little sauce, and you are done. The options
for tacos are endless, reflecting the country's infinite culinary variety.

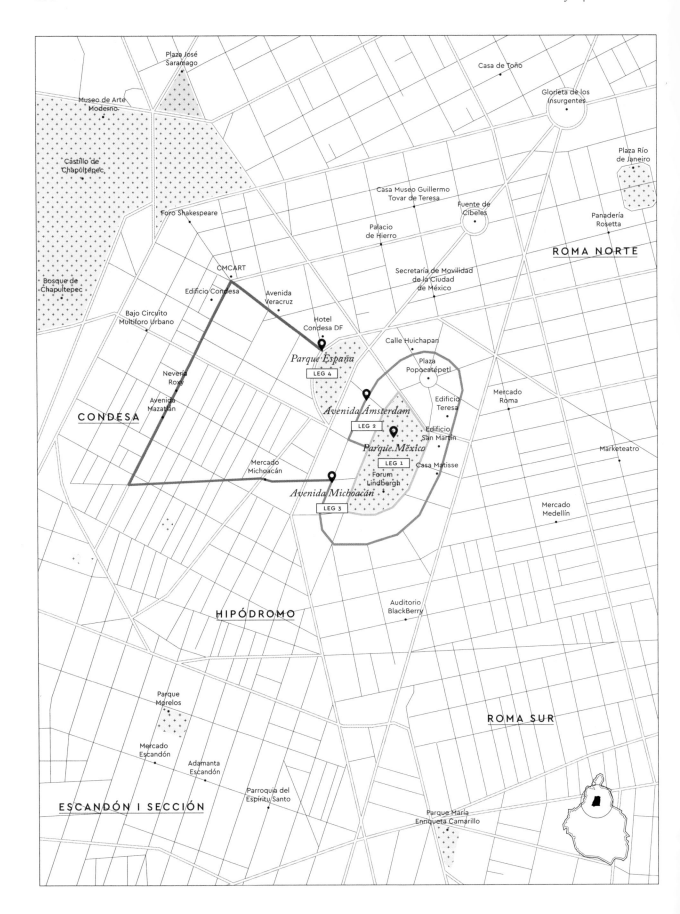

Plaza José Saramago

Casa de Toño

Museo de Arte Moderno

Glorieta de los Insurgentes

Castillo de Chapultepec

Plaza Río de Janeiro

Casa Museo Guillermo Tovar de Teresa

Fuente de Cibeles

Bosque de Chapultepec

Foro Shakespeare

Palacio de Hierro

ROMA NORTE

CMCART

Secretaría de Movilidad de la Ciudad de México

Edificio Condesa

Avenida Veracruz

Bajo Circuito Multiforo Urbano

Hotel Condesa DF

Calle Huichapan

Parque España

Plaza Popocatépetl

LEG 4

Mercado Roma

Nevería Roxy

Edificio Teresa

Avenida Ámsterdam

Avenida Mazatlán

LEG 2

CONDESA

Edificio San Martín

Marketeatro

Parque México

Mercado Michoacán

LEG 1

Casa Matisse

Forum Lindbergh

Mercado Medellín

Avenida Michoacán

LEG 3

Auditorio BlackBerry

HIPÓDROMO

ROMA SUR

Parque Morelos

Mercado Escandón

Adamanta Escandón

Parroquia del Espíritu Santo

ESCANDÓN I SECCIÓN

Parque María Enriqueta Camarillo

THE HEART OF COSMOPOLITAN MEXICO CITY

Watch your step! Trees and roots seem to have taken over in Condesa, much to the delight of locals and tourists, who can enjoy one of the greenest areas of the city between Parque México and Parque España.

LEG 1: EXPLORING PARQUE MÉXICO

A lovely place to chill, whether looking out over the lake, reading a good book, sipping a coffee while nibbling *churros*, or even doing some exercise. Alternatively, just sit on a bench and soak up the atmosphere. The Foro Lindbergh at the center, with its Fuente de los Cántaros ("fountain of the jugs"), is an ideal place to meet for a stroll. There are buskers, people selling all manner of things, and entertainment options wherever you look.

LEG 2: A STROLL ROUND ÁMSTERDAM

Avenida Ámsterdam is a distillation of the best aspects of Mexico City. Athletic types take advantage of its oval shape to jog, animal lovers walk their dogs, and foodies take a seat on a terrace and enjoy the shade of one of the most densely wooded boulevards the city has to offer. Despite the huge damage caused to the street by the earthquakes of 1985 and 2017, architects have let their imaginations run wild, combining Art deco stylings with more original creations such as the Casa Mondrian and Matisse, the famous restaurant.

LEG 3: A JAUNT ALONG MICHOACÁN AND MAZATLÁN

Other good locations for dining, going out, and exploring the city's impressive culinary offerings include Avenida Michoacán and Avenida Mazatlán, where the offices empty and the terraces fill up at the end of each afternoon. Call in at the Mercado Michoacán on the way for an incredible variety of fruit, vegetables, and flowers at very good prices, and choose between Mexican, Spanish, French, and Korean specialties at stalls just a few feet apart. The best way to navigate Mazatlán is in the shade of the immense trees of the central reservation, trusting your intuition to choose a *torta de chilaquiles* (sandwich filled with fried *tortillas* and doused in a spicy sauce), a craft maguey sorbet, or even a traditional guava pastry.

LEG 4: IN THE SHADE OF AVENIDA VERACRUZ

At the advent of spring, the jacaranda trees lining Avenida Veracruz burst into flower in a riot of purple that is both astonishing and short-lived, and it is then that *Chilangos* choose to take a stroll along this quiet avenue linking the bustle of Paseo de la Reforma with Parque España. Take time to enjoy the Porfirio-era façades from the last century and round off a sunny afternoon by ordering a legendary *carajillo* (a coffee with a shot of Licor 43 or sake) on the rooftop terrace of the Hotel Condesa DF and enjoying the view over the whole district.

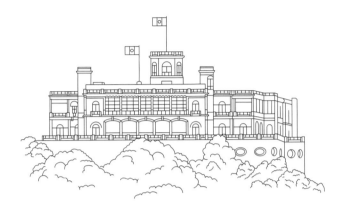

SAN MIGUEL CHAPULTEPEC

San Miguel Chapultepec, Tacubaya, and Escandón together form the so-called Tacubaya triangle, where you will find a jumble of local markets, stores, and architect-designed houses. The district is rediscovering some of its former splendor and has been the epicenter of contemporary Mexican art since the turn of the century.

P. 102

The area still has plenty of cantinas *among the architects' practices and art galleries.*

OPPOSITE

San Miguel has become a mecca for developers who demolish dilapidated housing.

Before the Aztecs arrived, Tacubaya was a fishing village of which traces have been found dating back to 1000 BCE. The area is now nicknamed the *Guerra des los Pasteles* (Pastry War) after events that took place during a time when Franco-Mexican relations were more strained; in 1832, some Mexican officers looted a store belonging to a French pastry chef in Tacubaya and, over the following years, other French nationals were even murdered. Louis Philippe I, the King of France, reacted by dispatching a fleet in 1838 to demand compensation on behalf of his subjects, but this French intervention was to remain fruitless.

The rise of the Tacubaya triangle began at the turn of the twentieth century, a time when Mexico City itself was experiencing impressive growth. Construction of the Ermita (the city's tallest building at the time) started in the 1930s and the Condesa Theater took up residence there. In 1947, the architect Luis Barragán built a house and studio here (Casa Luis Barragán), in which he lived until his death in 1988. UNESCO listed the house as a World Heritage site in 2004 and this masterpiece by the only Mexican architect to have won the Pritzker Architecture Prize makes a trip to the area worthwhile on its own.

The transformation of Tacubaya began when art galleries started to open at the turn of the 2000s. Many artists have found inspiration in its architectural heritage and wealthy families, attracted by its authentic Mexican atmosphere, have bought into this central district far from the hustle and bustle of its neighbors.

Escandón begins as you reach the other side of Avenida Jalisco with its creative, hand-painted signs denoting shoemakers, hatters, blacksmiths, and other workshops, taking us back into the last century. Everyone knows everyone and the few tourists who venture into this village-like area mainly come to enjoy this authentic experience.

San Miguel Chapultepec lies alongside the Bosque de Chapultepec. An incredible canopy of trees shades peaceful, residential streets that are best explored slowly, on foot. Contemporary art galleries alternate with architect-designed houses and concept stores (from wine bars to small grocery cooperatives) are flourishing in what is considered one of the capital's best-kept secrets.

THE ESSENTIALS

27

LABORATOIRE

Laboratoire boasts four floors of international artists at
56 Calle General Antonio León.

28

ARCHIVO DISEÑO Y ARQUITECTURA

This gallery opened in 2012 to promote Mexican and international industrial design with more than 1,300 works on display.

29

CASA BARRAGÁN

Luis Barragán's home and studio is an intimate journey through the work and life of the Mexican architect.

30

CASTILLO DE CHAPULTEPEC

Enjoy a 360-degree panorama of the capital from this castle, built on a hill in the Bosque de Chapultepec in the eighteenth century.

31

CASA GILARDI

This colorful, minimalist house is an architectural gem and was completed in 1976 as the last work of the renowned Mexican architect Luis Barragán.

32

MERCADO EL CHORRITO

San Miguel Chapultepec locals meet up at this small traditional market to eat lunch and stock up on supplies.

33

KURIMANZUTTO

This contemporary art gallery opened its doors in 1999 and is the largest in Latin America, with its range of exhibitions and cultural activities that is incomparable in Mexico City.

ABOVE

*Take care! Roots tear up the sidewalks with complete impunity
in the most heavily wooded area of the capital.*

OPPOSITE

*San Miguel's shady streets offer a perfect opportunity to explore the
area and its architect-designed houses on foot.*

With its metal furniture and hand-painted menu, La Chula on
Avenida Revolución recreates the traditional atmosphere of a local taquería.

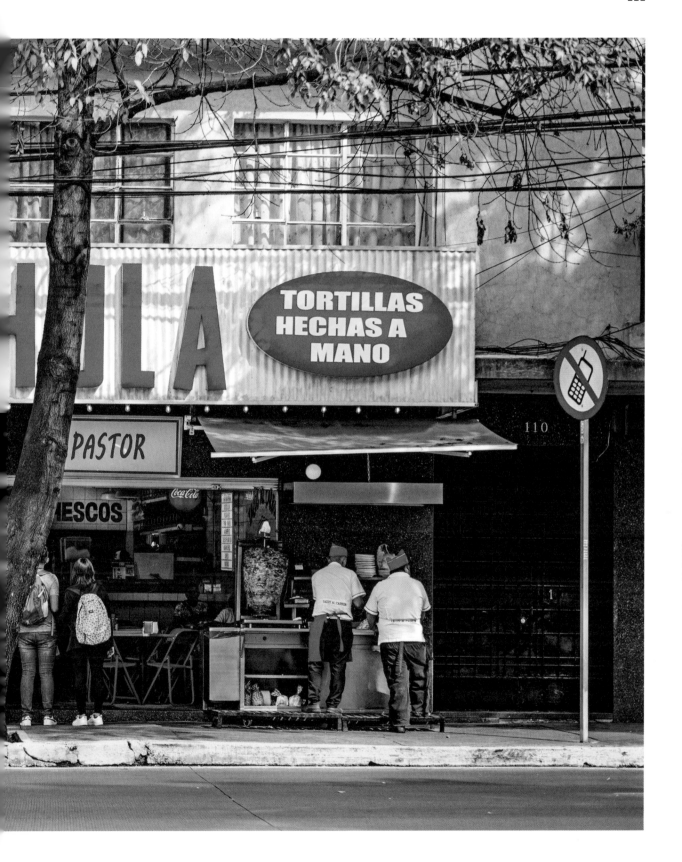

LIFESTYLE

CASA LUIS BARRAGÁN
THE ARCHITECT WHO PLAYED WITH LIGHT

The architect Luis Barragán (the only Mexican to win the Pritzker Architecture Prize, in 1980) designed and built his home and studio among the grocery stores, family-run restaurants, and craft workshops in the heart of Tacubaya.

No discussion about contemporary Mexican architecture is complete without mentioning Luis Ramiro Barragán Morfín, its greatest exponent. The name may be unfamiliar to some, but his immense, brightly painted walls in shades of pink or yellow are known throughout the world. Although hailing from Guadalajara (Jalisco State), it was in Mexico City that he fully expressed his creativity and found international fame.

With a passion for Mexican craftsmanship and French gardens, he drew particular inspiration from the French landscape gardener Ferdinand Bac, whom he met in Paris and who encouraged his enthusiasm for landscaping. Barragán made no distinction between architecture, landscape, and garden design, claiming, "to me they are one."

Barragán had one other love: the natural light with which he designed his spaces and painted his walls. His friend the painter Chucho Reyes advised him and helped him with choosing his colors, and the vast pink walls and orange on the roof of the house in particular are down to him.

Do not be put off by the scrappy appearance of the vast gray wall at 14, Calle General Francisco Ramírez; it conceals one of the city's most beautiful architectural gems. As soon as you enter, you are bathed in a soft, golden glow and the immense height of the ceilings almost makes you want to duck down as you pass through the comparatively tiny doors. The staircases are vertiginously steep and yet the whole thing seems to mesh together perfectly.

This might be due to the furniture, custom-made by Cuban interior designer Clara Porset. Or perhaps it is the simplicity with which the rooms are designed. Barragán is the spiritual father of Mexican functionalism. It might well be the infinite array of bookshelves, covering the entire wall of the sitting room and holding more than 2,000 volumes.

Barragán never explained the choices he made, constantly repeating that it was an architect's job to create peaceful spaces so that people could live out their spirituality and faith in silence, sometimes even with a touch of magic. Religion is an obvious element of the work of this fervent believer; crosses are a central feature on the walls and, even when physically absent, appear on the ground, where they are drawn with light and shadow.

At the age of 78 (in 1980), the famed Mexican
architect was awarded the Pritzker Prize
(the equivalent of the Nobel for architecture)
for the totality of his work.

ARCHITECT OF LIGHT

Minimalist architect Luis Barragán
has achieved global fame for his command of space,
voids, light, and color

ABOVE

The Volkswagen Beetle is affectionately known as the Vocho *in Mexico.*

OPPOSITE

The architect Alberto Kalach has turned an old carpentry workshop into the Kurimanzutto art gallery.

PORTRAIT

SANTIAGO MUÑOZ
THE TRADITIONAL ART OF CORN

You would be right to think that any self-respecting dining establishment in Mexico would have *tortillas*, the corn pancakes served with pretty much every kind of Mexican cuisine. There's a *tortillería* on every corner.

For Santiago Muñoz, it all started when he joined the crew at Nicos, a traditional Mexican restaurant, where he was taught how to make *tortillas*. "Before that, I just thought *tortillas* came from the *tortillería*," he admits with a smile.

It was also here that he learned nixtamalization, a traditional process that involves cooking the corn kernels overnight (and sometimes longer) in a mixture of lime and ash. He was seized by a passion for corn, which is often of very poor quality, even though it is so important in Mexican cuisine.

Santiago goes on to say that he finds it "sad, in a country where corn is king, that *tortillas* can be so bland and lacking in flavor and nutrients." He also remembers with a smile the evening on which he realized the poor taste of other *tortillas* after eating tacos made by his mother. He promised himself he would never eat bad ones again. "I'm a *tortillero* and proud of it!" He now hosts food lovers in what he calls "an experimental living space that is all about corn." His quest to find producers of corn *criollos* cultivated "with no human intervention," as purely as possible, led him to rediscover his country, in which more than sixty-four different varieties are grown. Above all, the twin impulses of curiosity and a love of food prompted this self-taught expert to leave his background in the hotel industry and turn himself into a chef, and then a corn specialist.

In 2015, Maizajo opened its doors, a multifunction space that is a *tortillería*, restaurant, taco bar, and experimental kitchen (all at the same time). The name comes from a variety of corn in danger of extinction that Santiago discovered at the national corn trade fair in Tlaxcala. He has made it his mission to bring corn into the modern age, from mill to *comal* (the steel or earthenware pot used to cook *tortillas*). He transforms corn into *totopos* (triangles of fried *tortilla*), *sopes* (*tortillas* with slightly thicker edges), *tlacoyos* (oval *tortillas* filled with cheese or black beans), and *gorditas* (circular *tortillas* that are filled and fried). His *tortillas* may be blue, pink, or white, depending on the variety of corn. Whether you come for lunch, to buy the *tortillas* of the week, or to explore the creations of the many chefs who are regularly invited to take charge of the kitchen, corn will always be center stage.

In sharing his love for his country and for Mexican culinary tradition, Santiago is honoring one of the most commonplace of products and restoring the humble *tortilla* to its former glory.

As evening falls, the *tortillería* is transformed into a taco bar and the terrace becomes a restaurant where corn and fine wines are served in perfect harmony.

INDIGENOUS CORN

Santiago Muñoz only uses heritage varieties of corn in the kitchen of Maizajo, his *tortillería*, and everything is grown in Mexico.

ABOVE

*The area, which has only recently been discovered by tourists, enjoys a simple
and traditional way of life in which local stores are of central importance.*

OPPOSITE

*The district is resisting the incursions of the big brands that have
taken over elsewhere in the city.*

DEEP DIVE

AGAVE

FROM PLANT TO ALCOHOL

Agave and Mexico are inseparable; no fewer than 159 types of agave grow on
Mexican soil, accounting for seventy-five percent of known species throughout the world.
These slow-growing plants are used in the textile industry and to make alcoholic drinks.

Pre-Columbian civilizations are known to have consumed *pulque* (which was known at the time as *octli*), a low-alcohol beverage reserved for religious and political ceremonies. Dubbed the "drink of the gods," this sweet nectar was made by fermenting the sap extracted from agave leaves and should not be confused with *aguamiel*, another pre-Columbian beverage, which was extracted from the heart of the plant.

Pulque had become a popular alcoholic drink by the nineteenth century, and this thick, whitish, sticky beverage (which was thought to have nutritional properties) was enjoyed in *pulquerías*, a kind of Mexican inn. As European migrants imported beer into Mexico, however, it began to usurp *pulque*'s place in Mexican hearts over the next century and *pulque* now continues to exist mainly thanks to low-volume craft production.

By the sixteenth century, the Spanish had begun to cultivate blue agave; the heart (*piña*) was then harvested and cooked, and the resulting liquor distilled, to obtain a beverage high in alcohol with a powerful aroma; they had invented tequila, one the most popular alcoholic beverages in the world! Industrial manufacturers later imposed a monoculture of blue agave and bottles flooded out onto the market international. Tequila was to become an icon of the country and a source of national pride. Its manufacture has been protected intellectual property since the 1990s and only the states of Jalisco, Guanajuato, Michoacán, Tamaulipas, and Nayarit are permitted to produce it.

Having largely been ignored by history, mezcal began its great comeback at the turn of the millennium. The manufacturing process is almost identical to that for tequila, but unlike the latter (which is produced from only one variety of agave), mezcal can be made from a hundred or so species, which can all be mixed together. The real difference lies in the distillation of wild species, however; these mature only after seventeen to twenty-four years and a far wider range of tastes can be achieved, but it is also far more difficult to obtain a consistent marketable product. Many mezcal producers have continued traditional production into the modern era, constructing immense temporary ovens on the ground in which the agave hearts are covered with earth and volcanic rocks and cooked for hours. This is followed by distillation in a copper still and aging in a glass bottle.

MAKING TEQUILA

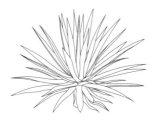

01

CULTIVATION

Blue agave reaches maturity
after seven years.

02

HARVESTING

The leaves are trimmed off
and only the heart, known
as the *piña*, is retained.

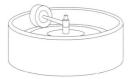

03

GRINDING

The agave hearts are crushed and
ground up to extract the juice.

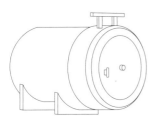

04

COOKING

The agave sugars are
cooked out to allow fermentation.

05

FERMENTATION

The agave juice is fermented
with yeasts for twenty-four to
thirty-six hours.

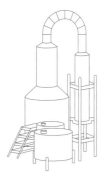

06

DISTILLATION

The alcohol is concentrated with
several rounds of distillation.

07

FILTRATION

Filtration guarantees the
quality and transparency of
the tequila.

08

AGING

Tequila *añejo* is aged in oak
casks for a minimum of
twelve months.

09

BOTTLING

The tequila is bottled and
distributed throughout
the world.

A SOURCE OF NATIONAL PRIDE

Although tequila undoubtedly remains Mexico's alcoholic drink of choice,
mezcal (which is made in almost exactly the same fashion) is attracting
increasing numbers of fans.

ABOVE

*Mexicans often stock up on provisions at markets where greengrocers and
butchers provide great value for money.*

OPPOSITE

You will find plenty of stalls selling freshly prepared snacks known as antojitos.

ABOVE

The streets around the markets are full of colorful trucks loaded with produce from the countryside.

OPPOSITE

You will find adverts for removals and logistics companies at every turn.

NATURE

BOSQUE DE CHAPULTEPEC

FRIED FOOD ON DEMAND

Chips and fries are usually sprinkled with lemon juice,
hot sauce, and a variety of seasonings.

2,000 ACRES (810 HECTARES)

This enormous park is three times the size of New York's Central Park.

FERRIS WHEEL

There is a funfair in the Bosque de Chapultepec, along with a dozen or so museums.

BOTANICAL GARDENS

The hothouse in the botanical gardens boasts an impressive collection of orchids and agaves.

360-DEGREE PANORAMA

Enjoy a view across the entire city from the terrace of the Castillo de Chapultepec.

CASTILLO DE CHAPULTEPEC

Once the home of Emperor Maximilian I, the castle is a piece of national history.

ARTIFICIAL LAKE

Locals take to the pedal boats on the large lake every weekend.

A MECCA FOR STREET FOOD

Visitors can look forward to sampling cotton candy, popcorn, chips, and all kinds of tacos.

FAUNA

While the squirrels lay claim to being the true tenants of the park, the zoo is home to giraffes, penguins, and a panda.

ABOVE

A helium balloon seller waits patiently outside a school.

OPPOSITE

Store façades make popular advertising spaces.

*Mexico City is one of the most congested places in the world,
with more than 5.6 million vehicles.*

*Pemex (Petróleos Mexicanos) has long enjoyed a monopoly
on hydrocarbons in the country.*

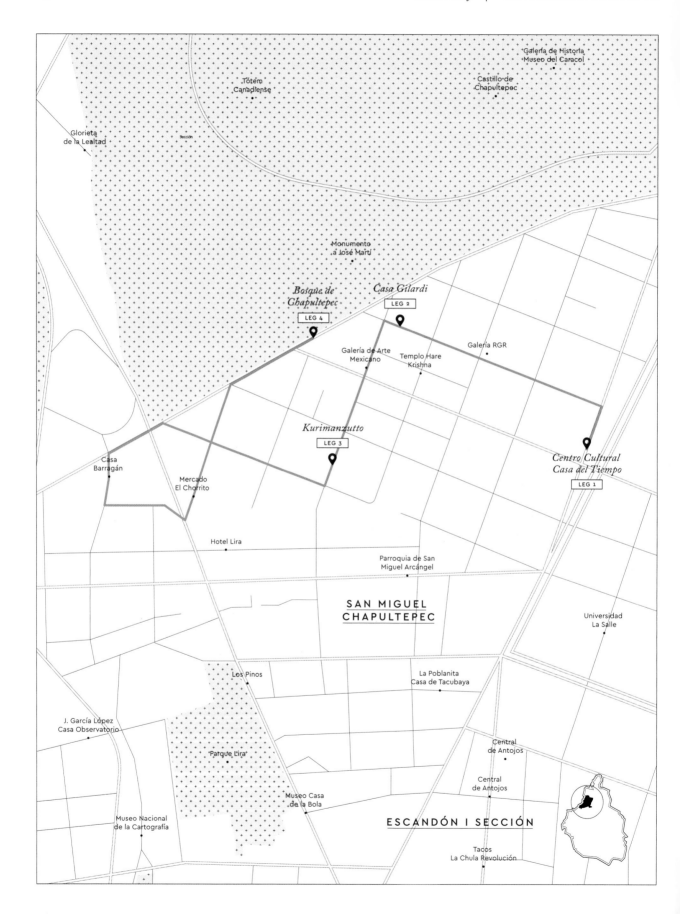

Galería de Historia
Museo del Caracol

Tótem
Canadiense

Castillo de
Chapultepec

Glorieta
de la Lealtad

Sección

Monumento
a José Martí

*Bosque de
Chapultepec*

LEG 4

Casa Gilardi

LEG 2

Galería RGR

Galería de Arte
Mexicano

Templo Hare
Krishna

Kurimanzutto

LEG 3

*Centro Cultural
Casa del Tiempo*

LEG 1

Casa
Barragán

Mercado
El Chorrito

Hotel Lira

Parroquia de San
Miguel Arcángel

SAN MIGUEL
CHAPULTEPEC

Universidad
La Salle

Los Pinos

La Poblanita
Casa de Tacubaya

J. García López
Casa Observatorio

Central
de Antojos

Parque Lira

Central
de Antojos

Museo Casa
de la Bola

ESCANDÓN I SECCIÓN

Museo Nacional
de la Cartografía

Tacos
La Chula Revolución

AVANT-GARDE ARCHITECTURE AND CONTEMPORARY ART GALLERIES

Though ideally located between Condesa and the Bosque de Chapultepec, San Miguel Chapultepec's peace and quiet meant that it long remained off the beaten track for tourists. Its art galleries have transformed this leafy district into a cutting-edge artistic hotspot.

LEG 1: ARTISTIC PROMENADE

A few years back, this area (one of the oldest in the city) was called Tacubaya. It was one of the liveliest parts of town, but peace and quiet have now descended and the art galleries have multiplied. One of the most iconic, the Galería de Arte Mexicano was founded in 1935 to exhibit works by Mexican artists from every era. The Galería RGR is more avant-garde, providing training for the artists of tomorrow and organizing artistic performances that are unique in their field. Just round the corner, opposite the Centro Cultural Casa del Tiempo, you will find a blue metal-roofed kiosk sporting the name RDD; this is in fact an independent publishing house producing reviews and art books as a cottage industry.

LEG 2: ARCHITECT-DESIGNED HOUSES AND CASA GILARDI

Calle General Antonio de León is home to one exceptional architectural creation after another, the best example of which is the Casa Gilardi,

Barragán's last commission, built with the sole precondition that the swimming pool and the jacaranda already present on the land should be retained. The outcome was astonishing, ultra-colorful pop art stylings. Other slightly more restrained edifices also do their imaginative best to turn this street into one of the most eclectic in the city.

LEG 3: KURIMANZUTTO AND CONTEMPORARY ART

As you proceed up Calle Gobernador Rafael Rebollar, look out for the discreet profile of Kurimanzutto, the largest and most important gallery of contemporary Mexican art, named after its founders José Kuri and Mónica Manzutto. The gallery was built by the Mexican architect Alberto Kalach using only concrete and wood, and it has exhibited some of the greatest artists of our time, including Gabriel Orozco and Damián Ortega.

LEG 4: FINISHING UP AT THE BOSQUE DE CHAPULTEPEC

The Mercado El Chorrito, located on the northernmost edge of the area between Tacubaya (where you can visit the Casa Barragán) and the Bosque de Chapultepec, is an excellent place to sample a few Mexican takeaway specialties such as *burrito campechano* (a wheat *tortilla* filled with rice, red beans, and a mixture of beef and pork) or *pastel de tres leches* (three-milk cake). The obvious place to try them is while relaxing on the grass or seated comfortably at a picnic table in the largest urban park in the Americas (1,695 acres/686 ha), although you risk the arrival of a gang of marauding squirrels.

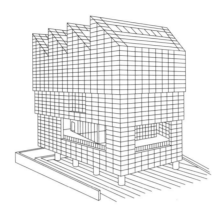

POLANCO

One of Mexico City's youngest districts is also its most exclusive.
Rents in Polanco are paid in US dollars and the standards expected by their
American big brothers are maintained. Luxury stores rub shoulders with
trendy museums and the capital is suddenly marching to a modern drumbeat.

Before becoming the economic heart of the Mexican capital, Polanco was a hacienda, an enormous stretch of farmland sold in 1920 to make way for a new district. It was ideally located just a few minutes from Centro, Condesa, and Roma, and soon became a refuge for the wealthiest in society, who came in search of security, green space, and a US lifestyle.

Large avenues perfect for cars and high society life, lined with immense colonial/California-style villas, were developed around Parque Lincoln and several other streets that were dubbed Polanquito ("little Polanco"). Bars and restaurants proliferated and by the end of the 1930s, the majority of the area was occupied by Jewish, Spanish, German, and Lebanese communities.

The 1950s saw the introduction of a functionalist style of architecture and the district, with its Conservatorio Nacional de Música, the Liceo Franco-Mexicano, and the Hospital Español was suddenly no longer a village. As the economic heart of the city, Polanco also boasts several luxury hotels along the Avenida de los Campos Elíseos, and many Mexicans saw these ultra-modern new buildings as proof of their potential to become a "first world" country.

The Museo Nacional de Antropología opened its doors in 1964 and, with exhibition space of nearly half a million square feet (45,000 m²), it is the largest museum in the country and one of the most comprehensive on the subject of pre-Columbian America. The Museo de Arte Moderno opposite opened the same year and exhibits twentieth-century Mexican painters and sculptors.

The 1980s witnessed a turning point for the area as it experienced an unprecedented real estate boom, with Avenida Presidente Masaryk becoming one of the most expensive streets on the continent. Three of the fifty best restaurants in the world (according to San Pellegrino's rankings) are in Polanco. Other recent arrivals include the Museo Jumex and its collection of contemporary art, along with the Museo Soumaya which exhibits an overview of Latin American art; the former is owned by a multi-million-dollar corporation and the latter by Carlos Slim, one of the world's wealthiest people.

The area is one of the safest, cleanest, and most prestigious in the capital and, although now the preserve of expatriates, rich Mexican families, and captains of industry, it is the perfect place to explore on foot.

THE ESSENTIALS

34

MUSEO SOUMAYA

This museum opened in 1994 to exhibit businessman Carlos Slim's private collection,
including dozens of sculptures by Rodin.

35

AUDITORIO NACIONAL

Concerts and shows are performed in this postmodern, brutalist building built in 1950.

36

MUSEO TAMAYO

This museum was built in the Bosque de Chapultepec in 1979 as a beacon of international contemporary art.

37

MUSEO JUMEX

This contemporary art museum owned by the Jumex fruit juice company boasts an eclectic collection.

38

CAFEBRERÍA EL PÉNDULO

El Péndulo is a café, restaurant, and bookstore with a wide selection of works in Spanish and English in pleasant and cozy surroundings.

39

SALA DE ARTE PÚBLICO SIQUEIROS

This small-scale museum exhibiting several frescoes by contemporary artists also houses the archives of the artist David Alfaro Siqueiros.

40

MUSEO NACIONAL DE ANTROPOLOGÍA

The largest museum in the country is devoted to the archeology and history of pre-Columbian civilizations.

La Ventana del Ticuchi is a culinary project inaugurated by
Enrique Olvera, one of Mexico's top prize-winning chefs.

NATURE

POLANQUITO PARQUE LINCOLN

SCULPTURE PARK

There is a permanent exhibition of many works by local and international artists.

EXCLUSIVE VILLAS

The park in this upscale and chic area is surrounded by large, lavishly decorated villas.

URBAN OASIS

The shade provided by the trees and the coolness of the swimming pools become essential as the mercury rises.

SQUIRRELS

The squirrels in the park show no signs of timidity and wait to be fed by strollers.

LOCAL LIFE

Fruit, vegetables, and fresh produce are always on sale every Saturday in the market in the Parque.

EXOTIC AVIANS

The birdhouse in the park looks after dozens of exotic fowl.

CALIFORNIA STYLE

Elegant, large-scale detailing, columns, and exterior molding are all typical of this style of architecture.

NEIGHBORHOOD STORES

As if frozen in time, small traders are the life and soul of the area.

MIRROR POND

The lakes in the park sometimes host sailboat races, to the delight of local children.

ABOVE

Despite all its modernism, some streets in Polanco retain an old-world charm.

OPPOSITE

*There are several dilapidated storefronts on Avenida Horacio,
such as this Kodak outlet.*

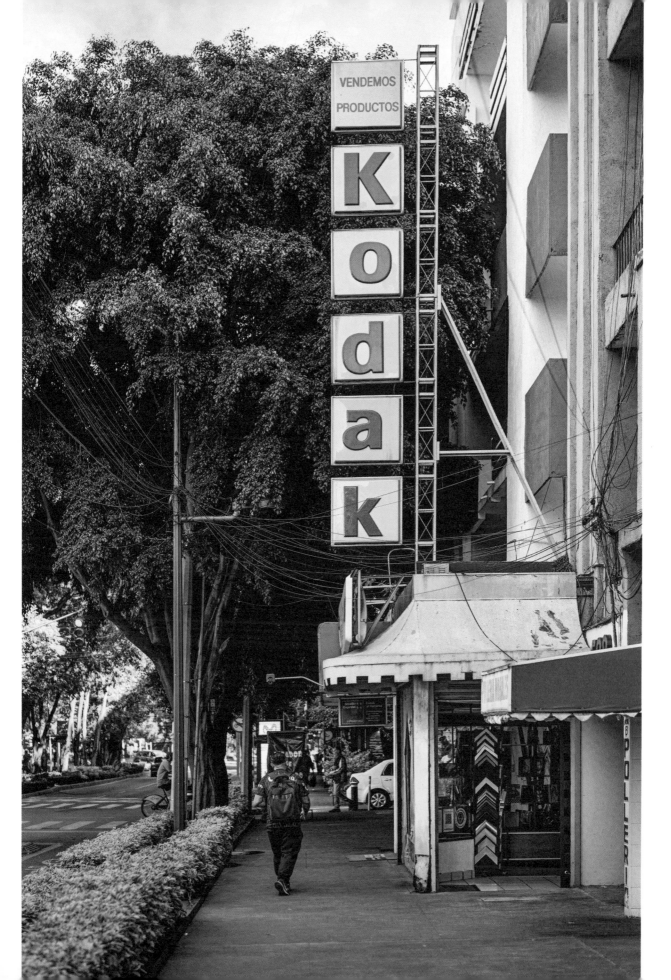

PORTRAIT

NEVERÍA ROXY

AN ICE CREAM AND SORBET BUSINESS HANDED DOWN FROM FATHER TO SON

The sweet scent of fruity sorbet and soda has been in the air in Condesa since 1946 thanks to Nevería Roxy, an artisan ice cream and sorbet shop enjoyed by young and old for more than seventy years.

When Don Carlos Gallardo and wife Doña María Luisa Rubio arrived in Ciudad de México, they decided to open up a California-style soda fountain. Their house special involved dropping a scoop of lemon-flavored ice cream into carbonated water; the ice cream sodas have always been homemade here.

The company is now run by Luis Gallardo, the founder's great-grandson, although he concedes he has to accommodate the wishes of his grandfather, who is still involved in the business and "doesn't want anything to change." Just stop at the corner of Avenida Fernando Montes de Oca and Avenida Mazatlán to see what he means; the paintings in the store are definitely from back in the day, as is the green and white striped awning.

Sitting down to a generous helping of chocolate banana split, Luis Gallardo relates that, when he was little, the sight of his grandparents spending their days handing out ice creams and refreshments to all the locals made him think of a career in ice cream selling. Years later, it was his desire to carry on a family tradition that prompted him to take over the reins.

Visit Roxy on a sunny afternoon and you will see grandparents bringing their grandchildren in after school, the same children who will one day return on their first teenage dates. As you might expect, the history of the bar reflected that of the city, with crazy evenings of dancing on tables, marriage proposals, 1980s rock'n'roll, and stars galore: the singer Enrique Guzmán, the daughters of ex-president Peña Nieto, actors from the sitcom *La familia P. Luche*, and the actor Chabelo have all been spotted at 89, Avenida Fernando Montes de Oca.

All of Mexico City has been through Roxy's doors, or rather they haven't, as there are no doors. Luis Gallardo tells us that his great-grandfather hated them, seeing doors as a social barrier that let some people in and "locked the others out." Roxy is, above all, a place for the people.

People come to Roxy for its top-quality ice creams, made with seasonal fruit from the Central de Abasto and the Mercado de Jamaica. The guava ice cream and delicious mango sorbet come highly recommended. People come for nostalgic reasons; having visited as children, they return for the sheer joy of it. Roxy has the sweet smell of remembrance of things past, filled with the flavors of yesteryear and stories to match.

The first Roxy outlet was on the corner of Avenida Mazatlán and Avenida Fernando Montes de Oca.

Erik Cruz welcomes customers to his store seven days a week.

Roxy was inspired by a 1950s Californian diner.

The store's original and unique creations are what make it so special.

Delicious cola ice cream float is on the menu.

Roxy has been part of the local furniture since 1946.

The original Roxy store has been renovated but still retains its old charm.

The red, white, and turquoise of Roxy is unmissable.

As in every other store, Our Lady of Guadalupe also puts in an appearance.

ABOVE

*The Carso business district is home to billionaire Carlos Slim's
various company headquarters.*

OPPOSITE

*Residential high rises and office blocks have shot up everywhere,
evidence of the crazy real estate boom.*

DEEP DIVE

CHILI PEPPERS AND *SALSA*
A LOVE STORY OF SAUCE AND SPICE

Salsa is a serious business; red, green, *tatemada*, *macha*,
slightly spicy or seriously hot, *salsa* is an essential element of Mexican cuisine
and is found in every dish, without exception.

Chili peppers have been a staple of Mexican cooking for more than 500 years, although they were already being cultivated and consumed by pre-Columbian civilizations 9,000 years ago. They were used as currency for a long time and the Spanish even demanded that some ransoms be paid in bales of chili peppers. They have remained one of the principal ingredients of Mexican cuisine to this day and feature in more than ninety percent of traditional dishes. They have even become a symbol of national identity.

The most popular variety is the *jalapeño* (fresh and green) or *chipotle* (dried), although all chili peppers are also called *chiles* in Mexico, from the Nahuatl word *chilli*. As the world's leading consumer of chili peppers, Mexico has plenty of other varieties, but beware of the *chile habanero* from the Yucatán peninsula; its diminutive size belies its status as the country's hottest chili pepper.

Although sometimes eaten straight (either cooked or raw), the condiment expresses all its true flavor and power when prepared as a sauce. Or rather as a *salsa*, and in Mexico, *salsa* is not an accompaniment but frequently at the very heart of the dish you are

enjoying. In Oaxaca, they make *moles* (a kind of curry/sauce) whose recipes list more than a hundred different ingredients and for which cooking times can vary from a few hours to several months, or even years! Different chili peppers can be grilled, peeled, boiled, blended, ground, or chopped before finally disappearing into a *salsa* that varies in color from fluorescent green to deepest black, including the most traditional orangey-red.

For octogenarian cook Doña Margarita Zaldivar Figueroa, the best way to receive guests "is to serve them a nice *salsa molcajeteada* to soothe their hearts and make their mouths water." This shows the importance of the *molcajete* (a kind of mortar and pestle usually made of basalt), which alone is capable of making a *salsa* worthy of the name.

Most dishes in Mexico are made with *salsa* in mind, and it features in everything from the simple taco to the most refined cuisine. Any self-respecting Mexican kitchen will also have not just one, but several dozen *salsa* recipes up its sleeve; there are officially 336, and it's up to you to find the one that tickles your taste buds and spices up your culinary explorations.

THE MAIN MEXICAN *CHILES*

FRESH CHILI PEPPERS

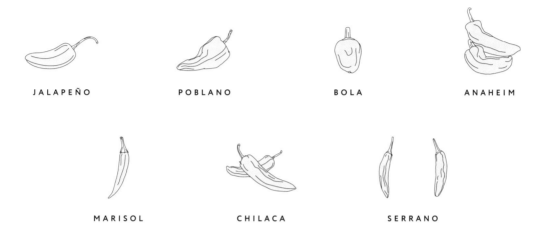

JALAPEÑO POBLANO BOLA ANAHEIM

MARISOL CHILACA SERRANO

DRIED CHILI PEPPERS

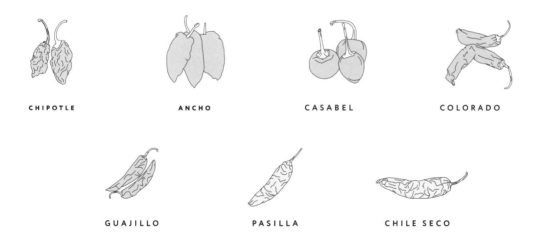

CHIPOTLE ANCHO CASABEL COLORADO

GUAJILLO PASILLA CHILE SECO

KEY INGREDIENTS

Mexican cuisine owes a great deal to these chili peppers, which are eaten fresh
or dried, whole or in sauces; they transform every dish into an explosion of
flavors (of greater or lesser heat!).

ABOVE

*Tree trunks are painted with lime as a protection from
abrupt changes in temperature.*

OPPOSITE

*Architects invested in the area during the 1950s to take the
pressure off the population close to the historic city center.*

ABOVE

*Everywhere you look you will find altars dedicated to
Our Lady of Guadalupe, some of which are elaborately decorated.*

OPPOSITE

*Polanco is a vast area with all kinds of architectural styles, inspired by
everything from colonialism to post-modernism.*

PLACE

PASEO DE LA REFORMA

FEELING THE PULSE OF MEXICO CITY

A stroll down the Paseo de la Reforma is a journey through Mexican history, from the independence declared in 1821 to the present day – an impressively modern Mexico City of skyscrapers and luxury hotels.

The Paseo de la Reforma extends for nearly 9 miles (15 km), crossing several districts and cutting an iconic swathe through the center of Mexico City to form an avenue lined with monuments and quintessential symbols of a country in perpetual flux.

The commission that began its creation was awarded to the Austrian engineer Ludwig Bolland Kümhackl by Emperor Maximilian, who reigned from 1865 to 1867, and the vast avenue was intended to link the Castillo de Chapultepec (the imperial residence) with the historic center of the city, in particular the cathedral. It was initially christened the Paseo del Emperador (or de la Emperatriz) before being renamed the Paseo de la Reforma in 1872.

1910 saw the installation of the Ángel de la Independencia on the avenue, a 120-ft (36-m) high column topped with a 22-ft (6.7-m) tall gilt statue of an angel that weighs 7 tons. The monument has now become a rallying point for all kinds of celebrations.

In 1942, it was joined by the Fuente de la Diana Cazadora, a monumental fountain on the first of many roundabouts that were installed on the avenue to improve traffic. The *Caballito* (little horse), an enormous (92-ft/28-m high) sculpture in garish yellow by the Mexican artist Enrique Carbajal González, was erected directly opposite the Museo Nacional de Arte (MUNAL) in 1992 to celebrate Hispano-Mexican relations, and the *Estela de Luz* (Stele of Light) was commissioned by President Felipe Calderón in 2012 to commemorate the bicentennial of independence and the hundredth anniversary of the Mexican revolution.

The tree-lined sidewalks teem with life, and street vendors and knick-knack stalls bring the atmosphere of a county fair to the vast avenue every weekend. The road is routinely taken over by demonstrations, parades, foot races, and other events, forcing motorists to sit in endless traffic jams.

Whether you are staying in one of its luxury hotels, dining on the top floor of one of its skyscrapers, visiting the Museo Nacional de Antropología, or taking a Sunday stroll or bike ride when the road is closed to motor vehicles, the Paseo de la Reforma provides a unique perspective on the lives of the capital's inhabitants and the history of the country.

Traditional dress and make-up to look like Catrina,
a character invented by the caricaturist
José Guadalupe Posada.

DÍA DE MUERTOS

The annual *Día de Muertos* parade takes over
the Paseo de la Reforma at the end of
each October.

ABOVE

Hammocks are a common sight in the capital.

OPPOSITE

*Patrons of the Lago Algo restaurant, an artistic and multicultural space,
can enjoy their food beside the artificial Lago de Chapultepec.*

ABOVE

Phone boxes are still in use in Mexico City.

OPPOSITE

*All the taxis in Mexico City were the iconic
Volkswagen Vocho until 2002.*

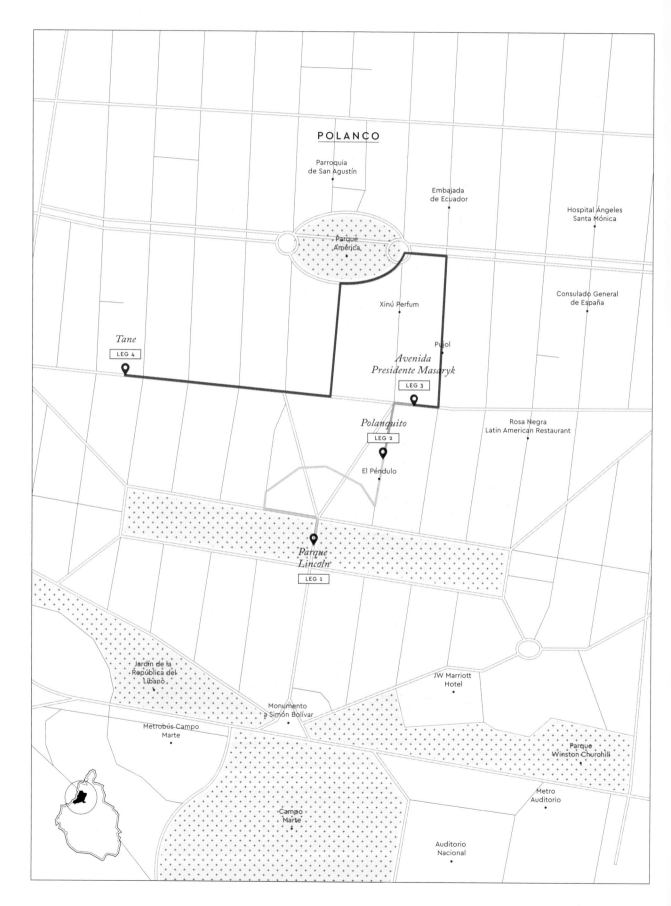

POLANCO

Parroquia
de San Agustín

Embajada
de Ecuador

Hospital Ángeles
Santa Mónica

Parque
América

Consulado General
de España

Xinú Perfum

Tane

LEG 4

Pujol

*Avenida
Presidente Masaryk*

LEG 3

Rosa Negra
Latin American Restaurant

Polanquito

LEG 2

El Péndulo

*Parque
Lincoln*

LEG 1

Jardín de la
República del
Líbano

JW Marriott
Hotel

Monumento
a Simón Bolívar

Metrobús Campo
Marte

Parque
Winston Churchill

Metro
Auditorio

*Campo
Marte*

Auditorio
Nacional

A SNEAK PEEK AT THE MEXICO CITY OF THE ULTRA WEALTHY

Polanco has a reputation as one of the city's most exclusive areas and is renowned for its embassies, award-winning restaurants, and luxury stores.

LEG 1: RADIO-CONTROLLED BOATS IN PARQUE LINCOLN

Begin your exploration of the area in Parque Lincoln, a small, rectangular green space surrounded by trendy restaurants and hugely expensive villas. The lake in the park is transformed into a children's paradise every weekend as kids gather to pilot radio-controlled sailboats; blink twice and you could be in Central Park or the Jardin du Luxembourg.

LEG 2: POLANQUITO AND 1970s CHARM

The pedestrianized streets north of Parque Lincoln have been nicknamed Polanquito and offer an infinite variety of culinary options, souvenir stores, and exceptional florists. They also boast some of the city's most beautiful book retailers, including the Péndulo café-bookstore. The slightly retro 1970s architecture lends the buildings a very particular charm and the slightly misleading feel of a seaside town. Its narrow Italianate streets and fountains are enough to drive out all thoughts of the noise, chaos, and immensity of the Mexican capital, at least for the duration of your walk.

LEG 3: STROLL ALONG MASARYK

With its luxury jewelry stores, French and American designer boutiques, and dealerships selling bulletproof cars on every corner, the Avenida Presidente Masaryk has long hovered at the top of the list of the world's most expensive avenues. Take a stroll to share in the lifestyles of the very rich and famous and discover a Mexico that is modern and proud (and perhaps even just a little full of itself). Although it may be difficult to find a taco *puestito* (stand), taking in this other Mexico from a café terrace is an experience to enjoy once in one's life.

LEG 4: WINING, DINING, AND WINDOW-SHOPPING

It's difficult to talk about Polanco without mentioning Pujol, the restaurant that has brought chef Enrique Olvera international fame and is now considered one of the finest in the world. Discreetly located at 133, Calle Tennyson, the country's most famous restaurant promises a voyage to the heart of Mexican culinary tradition. To round off your stroll, there is nothing to beat a trip to TANE for must-have Mexican jewelry; its immense sales floor, in violent pink (so typical of the Mexican capital) is a showcase for the silverwork that is one of the country's specialties.

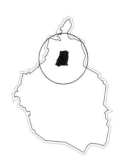

GENTRIFIED FRIVOLITY

JUÁREZ & CUAUHTÉMOC

Juárez and Cuauhtémoc are the epitome of trendiness.
Traditional grocery stores have given way to wine bars and cocktail lounges,
while concept stores and pop-up restaurants now attract America's gilded youth
as well as influencers from all over the globe.

These areas were among the first to be colonized as the city center expanded. Although the enormous Art nouveau-style villas are now interspersed with ultra-modern buildings designed by Alberto Kalach, a stroll past them is a journey through time. In 1864 Emperor Maximilian began construction of the Paseo del Emperador (now called Paseo de la Reforma) and it was completed three years later. This 9-mile (14.7-km) long major artery connecting Santa Fe to the city center passes the Castillo de Chapultepec and forms the border between the two districts.

Juárez and Cuauhtémoc were the first districts to be developed for the country's richest inhabitants at the end of the nineteenth century, and the Art nouveau villas constructed there now include several listed buildings. Over the years the area has become one of the most sophisticated and eclectic in the city as the toll taken by time and earthquakes has allowed its new architecture to take on all kinds of European and North American influences.

These historic buildings started a new chapter at the beginning of the 1950s, with restaurants, hair salons, and other stores breathing new life into what had once been essentially a residential area. The Olympic Games hosted by the city in 1968 gave the area a further facelift, and this was also when the Korean and Japanese communities moved in, bringing their culture and culinary customs with them.

In the 1980s the LGBTQ+ community used to congregate in what is now known as the Zona Rosa; as described by the Mexican writer Carlos Fuentes in *Where the Air Is Clear*, this city within a city is a nightlife hotspot with a somewhat notorious reputation thanks to its queer nightclubs, many sex stores, and the gay pride parade that attracts more than a million participants every year.

Juárez and Cuauhtémoc have the food trade to thank for a new lease of life enjoyed since the turn of the 2010s. Chefs from all over the world have been departing other districts (with perhaps over-hyped reputations for their culinary offerings) and taking over the area's historic buildings, transforming them into a creative hub of contemporary gastronomy in the space of just a few years. It was this culinary dynamism, largely of Korean and Japanese origin, that caused the *New York Times* to name the bustling area "Little Tokyo."

THE ESSENTIALS

41

ÁNGEL DE LA INDEPENDENCIA

The city's most iconic monument was unveiled in 1910 and
has become a rallying point for all kinds of festive events.

42

CICATRIZ

This café on Plaza Washington turns into a bar in the evenings, much to the delight of locals and tourists alike.

43

MERCADO DE ARTESANÍAS LA CIUDADELA

The stalls in this market sell handicrafts that pay exceptional creative homage to various national specialties.

44

QUERENCIA

A magnet for plant lovers, selling a wide selection of greenery to brighten interiors and balconies.

45

LIBRERÍA EXIT

The rare volumes sold by this art bookstore have made its name among lovers of beautiful books.

46

UTILITARIO MEXICANO

This store's unique products hope to promote Mexican craftsmanship and culture; the perfect place for souvenirs.

47

MERCADO JUÁREZ

A traditional market with open kitchens offering excellent breakfast or lunch options.

A bolero *cleaning and shining a customer's shoes
on the Paseo de la Reforma.*

Juárez's streets are named after major European cities.

PLACE

PROYECTO PÚBLICO PRIM

Just round the corner from the ultra-modern skyscrapers of the
Paseo de la Reforma in the heart of Juárez stand two buildings that have
resisted the vagaries of time, revolutions, and earthquakes.

Two rich families built immense villas here at the turn of the twentieth century, homes that were the epitome of contemporary luxury, with dizzyingly high ceilings and endless rooms decked out in marble and wood. The opulence of the Porfiriato, the authoritarian regime of Porfirio Díaz (1876–1911), was at its peak.

The Robles-Gil family lived at 30, Calle General Prim, one of the most beautiful buildings in the city, for thirty years, hosting fancy balls in which the debutantes of the era were presented to Mexican high society. The revolution gave such indulgences short shrift and the villa was summarily converted into offices, notably being used by the staff of the Cigarros La Tabacalera Mexicana, the national tobacco manufacturing company, before being abandoned in the 1970s.

The enormous villa next door at number 32, the home of the Capetillo and Servín families, suffered the same fate; after the revolution, it was divided up into modest apartments that were occupied until 2013, when the building was classified as a historic monument. At the turn of the millennium, the two derelict and partially dilapidated villas were acquired by Proyecto Público Prim, an artists' collective with an ambitious plan to preserve them and breathe new life into them. Taking on the not inconsiderable

challenge of conserving a piece of history without distorting it, the project to link the two villas and restore thousands of square yards of floorspace was an enormous undertaking.

The result is a real visual jolt, a leap back in time to an era of parties and luxury, but with one big difference: the louche residents of old have now been replaced with plants that climb up the walls and slink onto balconies, flourishing and spreading wherever you look. These have become the villas' new tenants. Monica Landa, the commercial director of the project, points out that greening the space was "a way of bringing living things to a place that at first blush might seem a little desolate, but was once bursting with life."

The Proyecto Público Prim is now trying to branch out; while the upkeep of the 12,000 square yards (10,000 m²) of the villas' floorspace is financed in large part by wedding hire and private functions, exhibitions of international art, emerging contemporary art fairs, and various concerts punctuate the always lively atmosphere.

The collective is also expanding its work and now hosts resident artists of all kinds, although there are conditions: their art must suit the place and they must donate one work to leave their mark on walls that already hold so much history.

Monsteras deliciosas (cheese plants) are just some of the green plants that have occupied the central patio.

Weddings and cultural events are held in the main courtyard.

The winter garden terrace is covered with native Mexican plants.

The tower blocks of the Paseo de la Reforma are a stone's throw away.

Try your hand at a variety of activities in the artists' studios on the second floor.

The winter garden is the best-kept secret in this enormous building.

The refined décor enhances the charm of the place.

The building is filled with antique and vintage furniture.

Take a culinary voyage in the Taverna restaurant on the ground floor.

Farmacia de Dios on Calle Río Pánuco is a local store selling
medications, beauty products, and perfume.

DEEP DIVE

SOBREMESA

AND OTHER MEXICAN CULINARY CUSTOMS

When they arrived in the Americas, the Spanish introduced customs that included the *sobremesa*, a moment of relaxation spent at the table after the meal is finished.

Europeans tend to finish a good meal with a strong coffee and a digestive liqueur, a tradition that has been continued to an extreme degree in Mexico, where it is not uncommon for the bottle of tequila to linger on the table.

Saturday dinners and Sunday lunches take up a large part of the day. Mexican waitstaff are reputedly the best in the world and are very attentive to diners, doing everything in their power to ensure that they have the best experience possible. Servers are paid through tips, so you should allow ten percent for normal service, fifteen to twenty per cent if you are very satisfied, and more if the experience was exceptional. It is not uncommon for mariachi bands (or musicians of all kinds), street vendors, and shoe shiners to put in an appearance, and you should certainly not expect peace and quiet. The background music will be loud and you will have to raise your voices to hear and be heard. Street life spills over into the restaurants and there is every chance of enjoying a few shots with your fellow diners.

As soon as you sit down at a table, you will almost certainly be brought lemon, several kinds of sauce, and *tostadas* (toasted corn *tortillas*) while you wait. Lemon is served "with everything" everywhere in Mexico, and you will also hear people say *con todo* when they order a taco, indicating that the taco will be served with onions and cilantro, two ingredients used almost systematically in traditional Mexican dishes.

As is generally the case in Mexico, people talk to one another in Mexico City whether they know each other or not. If you sneeze, you will be met with a sincere ¡*Salud!* ("bless you!"), and people leaving a restaurant will wish you a polite ¡*Provecho!* ("enjoy your meal!"). If it's your birthday, the entire world will join in with *Las mañanitas* (the traditional song on such occasions) at the tops of their voices, and don't be surprised if people ask you where you're from, what your name is, and whether you like tequila. The inhabitants of Mexico City are very proud of their city and more than happy to add their two cents to enhance the experience of those who visit it.

MARIACHI INSTRUMENTS

1 Guitar **2** Violin **3** Vihuela **4** Trumpet

Mariachi bands vary according to their geographical origins but will always have at least five members playing traditional instruments.

JALISCO MARIACHIS

During France's occupation of the state of Jalisco, the settlers used to pay musicians to entertain at their weddings, and legend has it that the term *mariachi* is a mangled form of the French word *mariage*.

ABOVE

A lavishly decorated altar to Our Lady of Guadalupe amid a riot of flowers in the middle of the Mercado de Artesanías La Ciudadela.

OPPOSITE

Some buildings constructed in the area during the 1930s are clad in traditional ceramic tiles.

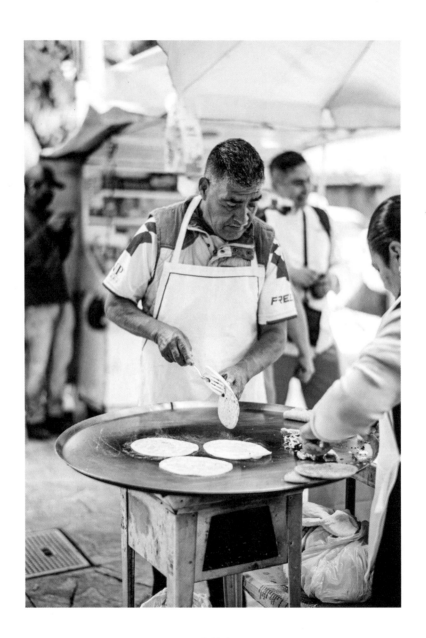

ABOVE

A puestito *selling* quesadillas *cooked on a steel* comal *in the street.*

OPPOSITE

Some new taquerías *have taken their inspiration from the old ones and offer an authentic experience, as does this one on Calle Río Guadalquivir in Cuauhtémoc.*

PORTRAIT

ENRIQUE MEDINA
CAFÉ *RICO*
AND AGROFORESTRY

Although coffee culture goes back to the eighteenth century in Mexico, locals have struggled to integrate a freshly roasted, caffeinated treat into their daily lives and instant coffee is still more popular, despite the fact that Mexican coffee is renowned for its quality and fine aromas.

Enrique Medina, director of operations at Buna, a company that produces coffee, discovered an interest in the bean by chance. Like many Mexicans, he had not been an immediate fan of a drink that some people find hard to love and only really encountered it when, not entirely of his own accord, he became a barista.

He then educated his palate and became interested in the art of coffee, until then a closed book to him. Specialty coffees were yet to be fashionable, but one thing led to another, and he now takes part in national and international barista competitions. After a chance meeting, he joined Buna, a fledgling coffee producer with great ambitions.

Coffee faces two challenges in Mexico. The first is economic, as the country is the tenth-highest producer of coffee in the world and yet almost all of its output is exported; from the state of Veracruz all the way to Chiapas, many families depend on coffee-growing. There are also ecological considerations, as coffee production is one of the most destructive ecosystems. Coffee-growing is also a very delicate process and the plants are often vulnerable to environmental disturbance and climate change.

There's no arguing with Enrique's conclusions, however: good coffee requires expert harvesting and a top-quality production process. Buna also promotes agroforestry by encouraging coffee producers to diversify their crops, in particular by introducing turmeric and ginger plants to their fields. Buna is no longer just a coffee seller, it has become a champion of Mexican ecosystems, leading the field in demonstrating that a fairer, more diversified, and more responsible system of production is possible.

Buna has been applying its approach to different kinds of farming, from coffee to chocolate and honey, always ensuring the same attention to detail and respect for the quality of the produce and the skills of the workforce.

To taste a proper *café rico* ("delicious coffee"), you will have to visit the Buna roasting shed and café in Laguna (172, Calle Dr. Erazo), an old textile factory that has been repurposed as a workspace for artists, young creative brands, designers, and architects.

Every stage takes place in-house at Buna,
from roasting to tasting.

MEXICAN COFFEE

Mexico is a major producer of coffee, with an impressive
wealth of experience that expands every day.

ABOVE

Shade from a fig or ash tree is perfect protection from the heat and sun.

OPPOSITE

There are plenty of people shouting in the streets; newspaper recyclers, scrap metal merchants, and vendors of water or gas.

ABOVE

*Partially abandoned and dilapidated buildings
rub shoulders with towers of glass and steel.*

OPPOSITE

*The Mercado de Artesíanas La Ciudadela, which specializes in
Mexican handicrafts, is surrounded by modern buildings.*

LIFESTYLE

ZONA ROSA

LITTLE TOKYO

Japanese and Korean communities settled around
Reforma during the 1970s.

SEX SHOPS

The Zona Rosa ("Pink Zone") was long known as the red-light district, but now attracts young LGBTQ+ Mexicans.

NIGHTLIFE

Partygoers enjoy the bars, nightclubs, and restaurants that stay open late.

SOUVENIRS

The area is now very touristy, with a wide variety of souvenirs on sale.

STREET FOOD

Hot dogs, tacos, and hamburgers are cooked on the street at all hours of the day and night.

FUSION CUISINE

Restaurants are increasingly combining their culinary influences.

ASIAN COMMUNITIES

Korean supermarkets import all kinds of exotic produce; it's foodie heaven!

A HINT OF EASTERN PROMISE

The area's large Korean community has its own customs and habits.

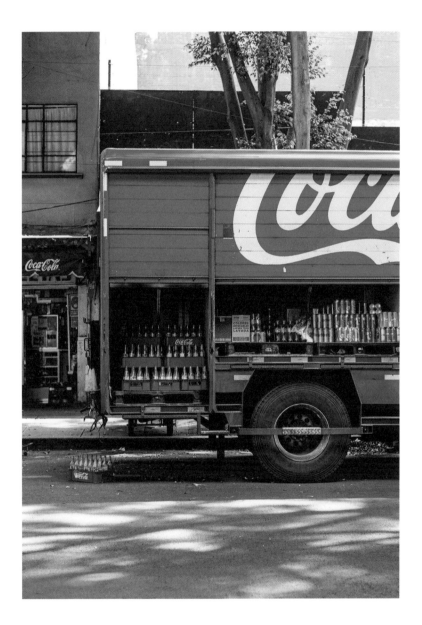

ABOVE

A delivery truck supplies the area's small grocery stores;
the country is one of the world's leading consumers of sodas.

OPPOSITE

Enormous villas from the last century eye one another
across the smart streets of Juárez.

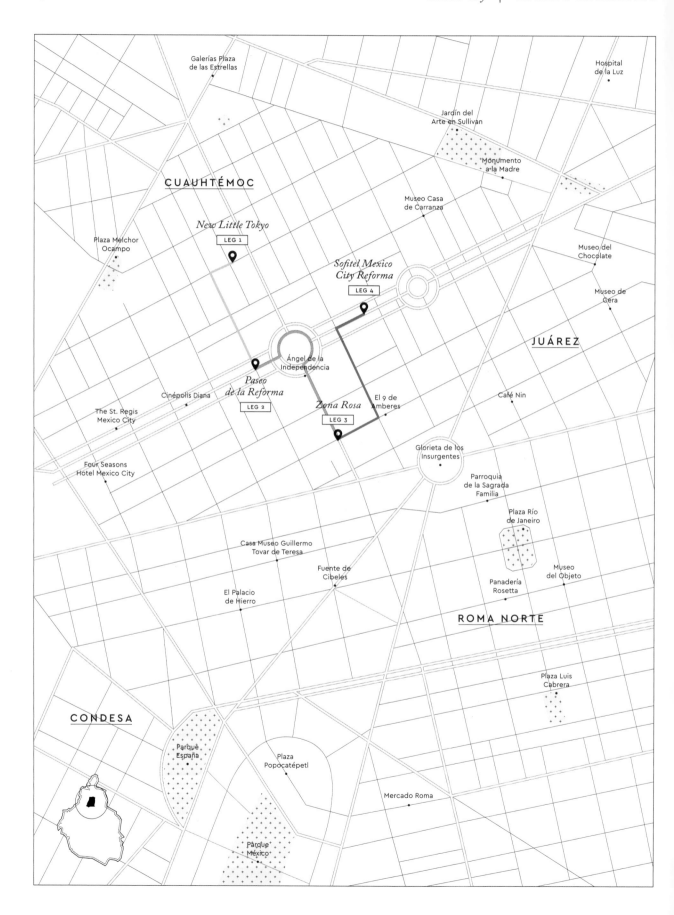

JAPANESE INSPIRATION, SKYSCRAPERS, AND THE ZONA ROSA

In the two cosmopolitan districts of Juárez and Cuauhtémoc you are most likely to bump into a mixture of *godines* (the nickname given to office workers on the Paseo de la Reforma), members of the Korean and Japanese communities, and passersby in the Zona Rosa ("Pink Zone"), the focal point of the LGTBQ+ scene in Latin America.

LEG 1: OMAKASE, MEXICAN-STYLE

The Calle Río Lerma was named after Mexico's longest river but has also been dubbed "New Little Tokyo," and for good reason; it seems that Japanese chefs of the greatest renown have been flocking to the heart of the Cuauhtémoc district to find inspiration since 2010. The *omakase* ("tasting menus") on offer in the *izakaya* ("bars") have given Mexican cooking a shot in the arm as they explore fusion options in which Japanese precision cozies up to Mexican creativity. Patrons are more than happy to knock back a few glasses of sake before retiring to one of the slightly insalubrious karaoke bars that abound in the area.

LEG 2: THE IMPRESSIVE PASEO DE LA REFORMA

The Paseo de la Reforma is a major artery and a symbolic thoroughfare that simultaneously divides the city geographically and unites its residents spiritually. At its southwest extremity you will find the imposing Castillo de Chapultepec looking out over its eponymous grounds, and as you walk toward it you will soon come across the *Ángel de la Independencia* ("Angel of Independence"), the icon of the city perched 150 ft (45 m) in the air atop a Neoclassical column. Nicknamed *El Ángel*, the monument was completed in 1910 and has become a focal point for national celebrations and demonstrations.

LEG 3: PARTY IN THE ZONA ROSA

El Nueve, Mexico's first gay disco, opened in 1974, and since then, the handful of streets that make up the Zona Rosa have established themselves as the beating LGBTQ+ heart of the whole country, perhaps even of all Latin America. The gay bars, sex shops, and most subversive nightclubs compete in inventive creativity, promising a crazy night that you won't forget in a hurry. Queer shows and celebrations of prides of every kind take place in one of the most cosmopolitan areas of the city.

LEG 4: BIRD'S EYE VIEW

The immensity of the Mexican capital can only be fully appreciated from above. Enjoy an incomparable view of the Popocatépetl and Iztaccíhuatl volcanoes from the thirty-eighth floor of the Sofitel hotel (when the thick veil of pollution lifts a little) and all the hotels along this Mexican Champs-Élysées have themed bars (with or without a view) where business travelers, curious tourists, and locals gather, leaving behind the city's clichés, without fear of heights, luxury, or earthquakes.

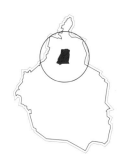

WHERE HISTORY AND CURRENT AFFAIRS MEET

SANTA MARÍA LA RIBERA
AND TABACALERA

Lying to the north of Cuauhtémoc, the aptly named
Santa María la Ribera, the oldest part of Ciudad de México,
was founded in 1861.

This district is said to have simply sprung out of the ground, with no urban infrastructure (electricity, water, sewers), but the wealthiest families wasted no time in settling here to escape the insanitary conditions and disease of the city center, and its streets are now some of the greenest in the capital, thanks to the many trees that have been planted.

The district expanded quickly during the twentieth century and new museums, stores, schools, and theaters appeared along its streets. In 1906 Porfirio Díaz ordered the creation of the Museo de Geología, an immense building dedicated to research and the sciences, and the La Cubana chocolate factory came to the area soon after, adding to the dynamism and growth.

The Kiosco Morisco, designed by the engineer José Ramón Ibarrola, was used as the Mexican pavilion for the World's Industrial and Cotton Centennial in New Orleans in 1884, and the Moorish-inspired kiosk has become one of the icons of a multicultural district that has been particularly affected by earthquakes and altered by gentrification.

Santa María lay abandoned by the end of the twentieth century after the city's wealthy families voted with their feet for new districts like Polanco, but the area enjoyed a new lease of life thanks to the architectural practices that reimagined nineteenth-century villas and transformed old factories into ultra-modern lofts. The result was astonishing, as a traditional, authentic Mexico that was almost frozen in time found itself rubbing shoulders with start-ups and contemporary art galleries that attracted a new and curious audience.

The district of Tabacalera a few blocks away has a similar story and takes it names from a former tobacco factory that has now been transformed into the Museo Nacional de San Carlos to house a collection of fine art. Not far away is the Plaza de la República with its Monumento a la Revolución, for which Porfirio Díaz laid the first stone in 1910. This mausoleum of heroes of the Mexican revolution was finally unveiled to the public in 1938 and has now become a symbol of the city, much like the *Cabeza de caballo*, the "horse's head" created by the sculptor Enrique Carbajal, a work installed at the end of the Paseo de la Reforma that has received love and hatred in equal measure.

THE ESSENTIALS

48

KIOSCO MORISCO

This kiosk was used as the Mexican pavilion during the 1884 World's Industrial and
Cotton Centennial and has become an icon of the district.

49

MUSEO DE GEOLOGÍA

This impressive museum was constructed in 1906 to house Mexico's largest collection of rare minerals and other precious stones.

50

SQUASH 73

This former squash court puts on exhibitions and cultural events throughout the year.

51

MUSEO UNIVERSITARIO DEL CHOPO

The German architect Bruno Möhring designed this palace of glass and steel in 1902 to house a museum dedicated to cinema and contemporary art.

52

EL ECO

A contemporary art gallery designed by the sculptor Mathias Goeritz.

53

CINE ÓPERA

Mexico's largest cinema was completed in 1949 and now has listed building status; it is currently waiting to be renovated.

54

FRONTÓN

The bastion of Basque pelota has been converted into a multicultural space that hosts concerts and exhibitions.

There are few large retail outlets here to compete with the small stores.

Traditional restaurants serve breakfast and lunch at very attractive prices.

ABOVE

*Everywhere you look in Mexico City, you will see old
American cars and traditional* Vochos *(VW Beetles).*

OPPOSITE

*Derelict buildings in this working-class area are often abandoned
before being demolished or renovated.*

DEEP DIVE

MEXICAN WRESTLING

Lucha libre ("free wrestling/fighting"), or Mexican wrestling, is a sport that has survived the passage of time and the vagaries of fashion to become a cultural treasure and a source of pride for an entire country. Its mixture of combat sport and staged sequences makes it one of the most interesting variants of the genre.

Wrestling is a Greco-Roman tradition, but certain Mesoamerican tribes (such as the Olmecs) had a similar practice for religious rituals and celebrations of important political events. It was not to reach its current form until the nineteenth century, however, when it was employed to entertain foreigners during the French occupation. Enrique Ugartechea is considered the first *luchador* and in 1863 he laid the foundations for what was to become Mexican wrestling.

Salvador Lutteroth, a former revolutionary lieutenant, created the Mexican Free Wrestling Company (Empresa Mexicana de Lucha Libre/EMLL) in 1922 and followed this up eleven years later with the opening of the Arena México, where masked Mexican wrestlers still face off to this day. It was around this time that Mexican wrestling became increasingly popular as it developed its techniques, acrobatics, rules, and folklore. Leaps into the audience, holds on the ground, and clever use of the ropes around the ring together built the legends of the first wrestlers.

El Santo, Blue Demon, and El Rayo de Jalisco all became stars of the big screen in the 1950s, filling arenas and movie theaters and contributing to a golden age of Mexican cinema in which they achieved legendary status. They made a fortune from merchandising and were unable to leave the house without donning their signature mask.

Most of the wrestlers are masked and the greatest defeat, and ultimate humiliation, is to be unmasked to the crowd. Once unmasked, a wrestler can never replace it and becomes a *caballera* ("one without a mask"). It is not uncommon to see the children of wrestlers adopt the family colors and continue a tradition that is now solidly established in popular culture.

Traditionally, two teams face off and fight: the *Técnicos* (who are more technical fighters, more respectful, and with a greater sense of fair play) and the *Rudos* (who are more violent and less deferential). The real action takes place not in the ring, however, but in the hall; insults and altercations are standard between fans and athletes and anyone sitting in the front row will find themselves drawn in (willingly or otherwise) as participants in a spectacle that may be kitsch but is incredibly entertaining.

EL SANTO
(1917-1984)

A *lucha libre* legend and
movie actor.

BLUE DEMON
(1922-2000)

Blue made a major contribution to
the golden age of Mexican cinema.

HURACÁN RAMÍREZ
(1926-2006)

The youngest of four brothers,
all of them wrestlers.

RAYO DE JALISCO
(1932-2018)

One of the greatest wrestlers of
his generation.

MIL MASCARAS
(1942)

A star who wrestled in Mexico,
the United States, and Japan.

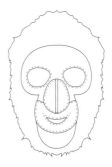

KEMONITO
(1967)

The darling of the *Chilango* crowd
and a *lucha libre* manager.

THE MASKS OF THE MOST FAMOUS WRESTLERS

These shiny, colorful, and iconic masks made a huge contribution to the
success of Mexican *lucha libre* in movie theaters and live performances, but
there is no greater humiliation than being unmasked during a bout.

ABOVE

Local residents have placed flowers on a small altar to
Our Lady of Guadalupe on the corner of a street.

OPPOSITE

The façades are coated with colorful waterproof paint,
in stark contrast to the gray of the rest of the city.

*An old pick-up parked in front of the Kiosco Morisco
near the Alameda de Santa María.*

PLACE

MONUMENTO A LA REVOLUCIÓN

A DISTILLATION OF MEXICAN HISTORY

President Porfirio Díaz announced an international architecture competition in 1897 to commission the construction of the Palacio Legislativo, a vast palace that would house the country's legislative machinery, including the Senate, the parliamentary chamber, various government agencies, and other official bodies.

The competition winner was the French architect and painter Émile Bénard. Having notably helped Charles Garnier create the Opera House in Paris, he went on to design a magnificent Neoclassical building for Mexico City, with more than 150,000 square feet (14,000 m²) of floorspace. The Mexican revolution, led among others by Emiliano Zapata and Pancho Villa, held up construction for many years, putting a stop to Porfirio Díaz's dreams of grandeur. By 1912 only the metal frame and central cupola had been built as evidence that the project had ever existed.

In 1933 the Mexican architect Carlos Obregón Santacilia reimagined Bénard's work as a building to pay homage to the Mexican revolution and buttressed the copper-covered cupola (a nod to the mines that had been the source of New Spain's wealth) with four immense pillars representing the country's founding principles: independence, reform, agrarian legislation, and workers' rights. An edifice initially conceived as a symbol of the might of Porfirio Díaz's government became a mausoleum dedicated to the heroes of the revolution.

The colossal Monumento a la Revolución is 220 ft (67 m) in height and visitors can roam the foundations of the enormous building to explore the various (and sometimes quite chaotic) stages of its construction. The building is both a museum and a mausoleum, and the remains of numerous revolutionary heroes lie interred in the crypts located beneath the four pillars, including Venustiano Carranza, Francisco I. Madero, Plutarco Elías Calles, Pancho Villa, and Lázaro Cárdenas.

After a facelift and renovation to celebrate the centenary of the Mexican revolution in 2010, the Monumento a la Revolución now offers one of the best panoramas of the city from its viewing platform, which is accessible via a glass elevator. A frisson of history is guaranteed, possibly along with vertigo.

1 / AN ODE TO THE REVOLUTION

This massive monument is an impressive and majestic tribute to the Mexican people and its revolutionaries.

2 / ENGINEERING PROWESS

The cutting-edge steel frame supports several tons of stone in an astonishing achievement of technical daring.

3 / MODERNITY

The monument has reinvented itself to the delight of visitors who enjoy its glass-floored panoramic elevator and interactive museum.

4 / MUSEUM

A journey through the history and development of the Mexican revolution awaits in the monument's cellar and superstructure.

5 / COPPER CUPOLA

The copper cupola pays homage to the Mexican mining industry and its unique expertise.

ABOVE

*There are vast parking lots everywhere, underlining
the importance of cars in getting around the city.*

OPPOSITE

*Gentrification has not spared this district, which has
become a magnet for real estate developers.*

*Mexicans are not shy about self-promotion and are happy to shout
their wares from the rooftops, or at least write them on the walls.*

OPPOSITE

*A small, tranquil, and colorful street is a reminder that
Santa María is mainly residential.*

PORTRAIT

LUIS ENRIQUE DE LA REGUERA

CRAFT BREWING IN CORONA COUNTRY

The craft beer revolution that first happened in the United States in 2010 has reached Mexico, and Luis Enrique began his own brewing journey by creating the Cervecería Cru Cru. Much more than simply a brewery, however, it's a cultural space that brings people together.

Foam flows freely in Corona country; Mexico is the world's fourth biggest producer of beer and the greatest global exporter, with two corporations (Modelo and Cuauhtémoc) carving up a lucrative market between them. Nothing in Mexico that would predispose its inhabitants to make beer, however; the country grows no malt of its own and the locals only started to drink the brew at the end of the nineteenth century. Despite this, Mexican beers enjoy an international reputation and are drunk on every conceivable occasion.

Luis Enrique de la Reguera is one of the cofounders of the Cervecería Cru Cru (8, Callejón de Romita), a craft brewery that is Mexican through and through and produces unparalleled numbers of prize-winning beers. The project began with a group of friends with the conviction that they could achieve their dreams and create their own beer within the framework of a socially committed, cultural, and artistic enterprise.

The Cru Cru brewery was set up in premises that had at different times functioned as a monastery, a middle-class villa, and even a set for a Luis Buñuel film (*The Young and the Damned*, 1950). Luis Enrique tells us that the name is a tribute to the call of the cricket, which is also the brand's logo and the emblem of the Bosque de Chapultepec (*chapul* means "grasshopper" in Nahuatl).

Luis Enrique aspires to imbue the beers he makes with Mexican expertise and tradition, creating brews like his interpretation of Germany's Gose, a beer lightly infused with *sal de gusano* ("worm salt") and *chapuline* ("grasshopper") extract, known simply as Gose con Chapulines. Cru Cru has also attracted attention for the creativity of its seasonal offerings, such as its Berliner with *xoconostle* (a kind of prickly pear) and hibiscus blossom.

Luis Enrique maintains that beer is the least elitist drink and as the favorite drink of the poorest and richest alike, it has the power to bring a whole country together. On a local level, the brewery unites the residents of Romita, the oldest district of Roma, around unique beers, while also offering *salsa* courses, ceramics workshops, and contemporary art exhibitions in a unique setting.

CRAFT BREWING

In producing an alternative to traditional Corona, Cru Cru is swimming against the tide in a country of industrialized brewing.

FILLED WITH LIFE

Salsa school, art studio, ceramics workshop: Cru Cru is not just a brewery, but also a lively meeting place.

ABOVE

Lush vegetation provides a stark contrast to the façades
of the skyscrapers lining the Paseo de la Reforma.

OPPOSITE

The Reforma 27 tower block (2010) designed by Alberto Kalach
is evidence of the desirability of this long-forgotten district.

LIFESTYLE

ARTISTS' STUDIOS AT LA CALERA

ARTIST IN RESIDENCE

La Calera provides young creatives from around
the world with a workspace for several months.

INTERNATIONAL

Artists from Latin America, Asia, and Europe live together in a unique space.

ART GALLERY

Exhibitions and events are organized regularly.

CULTURAL CENTER

Creative workshops for children and movie screenings have breathed life into the place.

HISTORIC PREMISES

The house at 62, Calle Dr. Atl has been playing host to all kinds of artists and writers since 1950.

ARCHITECTURE

A series of renovations has managed to preserve the charm of this unique building.

POSSIBILITIES

Santa María attracts and inspires young creatives from around the world.

A WELL-KEPT SECRET

La Calera is a secluded and little-known bastion of Mexican art.

Detailing in the local ironwork bears witness to a tradition of
craftsmanship that lives on proudly to this day.

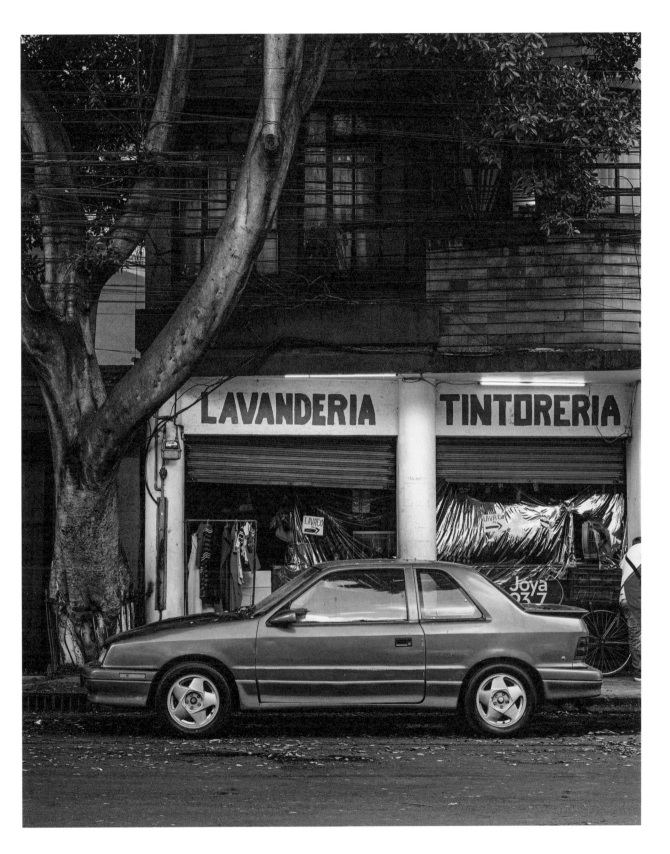

A laundry in the shade of an ahuehuete *(Montezuma cypress)*
reinforces the district's village feel.

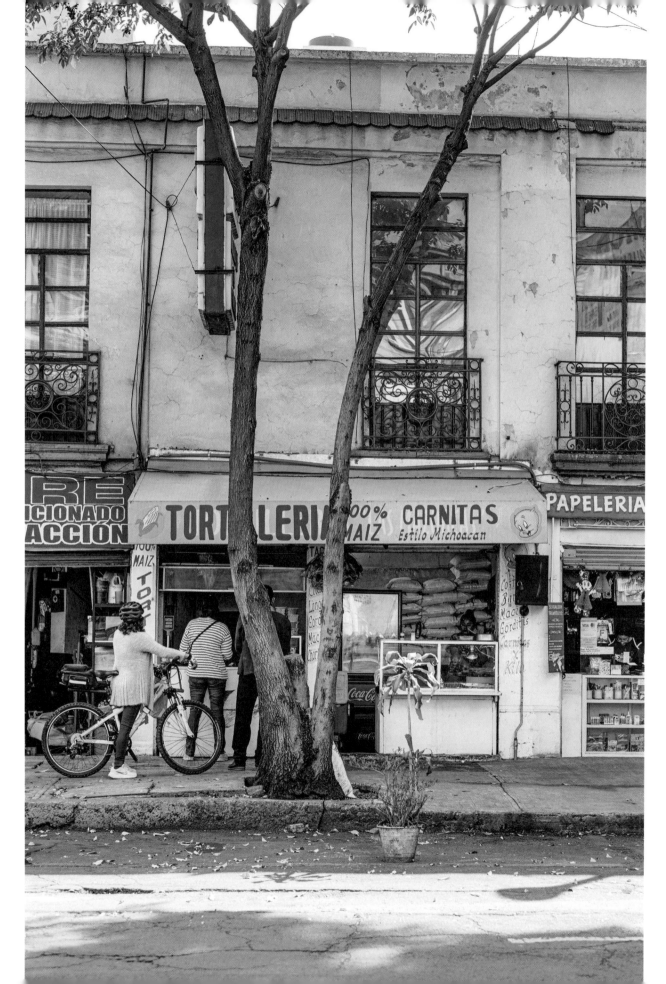

ABOVE

A man enjoying an antojito *on the go in the middle of a street.*

OPPOSITE

Small stores like these, repairing domestic appliances, making tortillas, *and selling stationery are an integral part of the local atmosphere.*

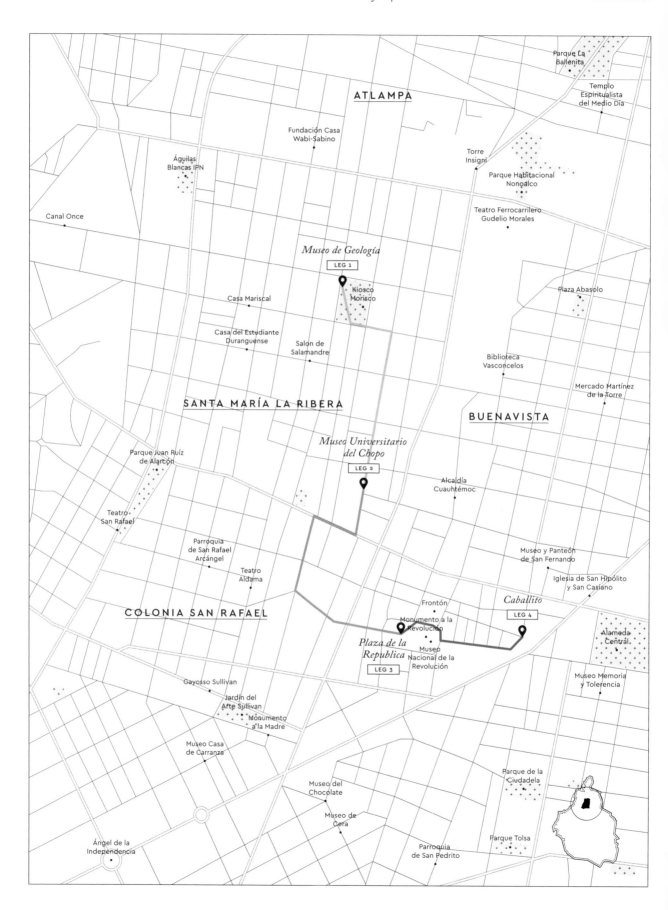

ATLAMPA

Fundación Casa
Wabi-Sabino

Águilas
Blancas IPN

Canal Once

Parque La
Ballenita

Templo
Espiritualista
del Medio Día

Torre
Insigni

Parque Habitacional
Nonoalco

Teatro Ferrocarrilero
Gudelio Morales

Museo de Geología
LEG 1

Kiosco
Morisco

Casa Mariscal

Plaza Abasolo

Casa del Estudiante
Duranguense

Salon de
Salamandre

Biblioteca
Vasconcelos

SANTA MARÍA LA RIBERA

Mercado Martínez
de la Torre

BUENAVISTA

*Museo Universitario
del Chopo*
LEG 2

Parque Juan Ruíz
de Alarcón

Alcaldía
Cuauhtémoc

Teatro
San Rafael

Parroquia
de San Rafael
Arcángel

Museo y Panteón
de San Fernando

Iglesia de San Hipólito
y San Casiano

Teatro
Aldama

COLONIA SAN RAFAEL

Frontón

Monumento a la
Revolución

Caballito
LEG 4

Alameda
Central

*Plaza de la
Republica*
LEG 3

Museo
Nacional de la
Revolución

Museo Memoria
y Tolerencia

Gayosso Sullivan

Jardín del
Arte Sullivan

Monumento
a la Madre

Museo Casa
de Carranza

Parque de la
Ciudadela

Museo del
Chocolate

Museo de
Cera

Parque Tolsa

Ángel de la
Independencia

Parroquia
de San Pedrito

AUTHENTIC AND REVOLUTIONARY MEXICO

Even as recently as a few years ago, the names of Santa María la Ribera and Tabacalera were little known, but major urban investment has gradually transformed these districts into tranquil havens where the authenticity of the Mexico of yesteryear flirts with modernity.

LEG 1: KIOSCO MORISCO

Our stroll begins in the shadow of the Moorish kiosk built to represent Mexico at the World's Industrial and Cotton Centennial in 1884. It is now a strategic rallying point where Mexicans come to play, read, hold demonstrations, and put on exhibitions. The Museo de Geología (1906) is opposite, most famous for its impressive double staircase.

LEG 2: CINEMATOGRAPHIC CULTURE AT EL CHOPO

The Museo Universitario del Chopo, another major cultural venue, first saw the light of day in an old pavilion built for the Exhibition of 1902 before being purchased and reassembled in Mexico City the following year. This structure combines metal beams and immense skylights and is now both a focal point of Mexican cinema and one of the most controversial museums because of its socially committed and avant-garde exhibitions, which invariably hit the headlines.

LEG 3: EVENTS, REVOLUTION, AND ROOFTOPS

Redeveloped in 2010, the Plaza de la República in the heart of Tabacalera is the epicenter of the history of the revolution and the Mexican trade union movement. Your eyes will be fixed on the imposing Monumento a la Revolución, with its four carved stone pillars and copper cupola, although the Museo Nacional de la Revolución just nearby is equally impressive. There is more than a whiff of revolution in the air of these streets where Che Guevara, Fidel Castro, and Pablo Neruda once lived, and not without reason as the headquarters of the Ferrocarrileros Mexicanos and Electricistas Mexicanos unions are adorned with some of the most important mural paintings in the country.

LEG 4: PASEO DE LA REFORMA

Leave the Plaza de la República and the impressive Frontón building (where Basque pelota was once played) behind you and you will reach the Paseo de la Reforma. This intersection at the heart of the four most central districts is a cultural and architectural melting pot where the *godines* (the nickname given to local office workers) in their three-piece suits, stock exchange traders, tourist buses, and the several million inhabitants of the city center all rub shoulders just across from the *Caballito* (the "little horse" designed by Enrique Carbajal) in the shade of high-rise blocks as iconic as El Moro (the headquarters of the national lottery), SAT (the Mexican inland revenue service), and the luxury hotels that stretch all the way to the Bosque de Chapultepec at the far end of the avenue.

COYOACÁN

AND THE SOUTH SIDE OF THE CITY

Before the Spanish Conquest, Coyoacán was a small village called
Coyohuacán ("the place where there are coyotes," in Nahuatl).
Such canines are notable by their absence these days, and the district
has gradually morphed into the city's artistic and bohemian quarter.

P. 2 2 8

*Coyoacán is known for its large homes with
unassuming exteriors and lush gardens.*

OPPOSITE

*The volcanic stone cobblestones give the area the distinct
feel of a bucolic, colonial village.*

It's impossible to talk about Coyoacán without mentioning Frida Kahlo. The most
famous Mexican artist in the world lived in the Casa Azul ("The Blue House") for
many years and it is now a museum devoted to her work. She had a gift for painting
and sharing Mexican folklore, crafts, nostalgia, and festivals, and the local area is
very much like her house/museum: colorful, festive, shady, and highly traditional.

Strolling through Coyoacán's small streets, getting lost in its parks, or lingering for
a moment in one of the area's many squares is rather like traveling back in time, as
modernity and tradition suddenly merge into one. The bars and restaurants still serve
traditional *pulque* and homemade hot chocolate, and street sellers and artisans tout
all kinds of treats and souvenirs. Dancing in traditional costume is often organized
and for a moment a city of more than twenty-two million inhabitants resembles a
country village.

Coyoacán is also not without culture. It has dozens of museums, including Leon
Trotsky's former home (where he was assassinated by a Russian anarchist in 1940)
and, a few streets away, the impressive Cineteca Nacional, the work of architect
Manuel Rocha Díaz. The building was completed in 1984 and renovated in 2012 by
Michel Rojkind, another architect, to house no fewer than ten screening rooms and
Mexico's largest collection of movie archives. The Fonoteca Nacional is a paradise
for music fans and a proud exponent of the works of great Mexican composers and
musicians such as Manuel María Ponce and Armando Manzanero.

To the south you will find the Universidad Nacional Autónoma de Mexico (UNAM).
This immense academic complex completed in 1910 is a hub of universities, research
centers, museums, libraries, and sports facilities, and even boasts a nature reserve.
UNAM has a reputation as one of the best Spanish-speaking universities and is the
alma mater of a host of Latin American intellectuals, politicians, and artists.

The district of Xochimilco at the far southern extremity of the Mexican capital has
an ecosystem that is unique in the world: a 410-acre (165-ha) lake, crisscrossed by
canals separating *chinampas*, artificial islands on which the Aztecs invented the
forerunner of hydroponic agriculture, a system still in use to this day.

THE ESSENTIALS

55

CASA AZUL

Frida Kahlo called this house/museum home for a large part of her life,
and there is an exhibition of some of her works and possessions.

56

CENTRO NACIONAL DE LAS ARTES

This center for higher education and culture was designed by the architect Ricardo Legorreta and boasts an arthouse cinema and an exhibition hall.

57

BIBLIOTECA CENTRAL

UNAM's central university library opened its doors in 1956 as the country's main public library.

58

MUAC

This university museum of contemporary art located in UNAM's Ciudad Universitaria has played host to exhibitions of international stature.

59

CASA ESTUDIO DIEGO RIVERA Y FRIDA KAHLO

The artist Diego Rivera's house was built by the architect Juan O'Gorman in 1931 and is made up of two studios connected by an exterior bridge.

60

CINETECA

The Cineteca Nacional opened its doors in 1974 and its ten screening rooms are dedicated to arthouse and experimental cinema.

61

LOS VIVEROS

This national park has been a green haven since 1907, and there are plenty of flower and plant sellers here.

A Día de Muertos *altar decorated with photos of the deceased,* cempasúchile *(Mexican marigold) petals, offerings, and candles.*

The often colorful façades of the buildings contrast with the local volcanic stone.

DAFNE TOVAR
CREATING STORIES IN FLOWERS

We catch up with Dafne Tovar at the entrance to the Mercado Jamaica, one of the best-stocked and most astonishing markets in the whole of Latin America, famous for its range of flowers. She is a regular here and is soon greeted by the sellers as she strolls through its aisles.

Dafne Tovar is entirely self-taught, but her sensitivity in dreaming up the flower arrangements that have made her reputation is a rare gift. In 2013 she said farewell to the gray world of office administration to pursue her new passion; she tells us that she often used to come to the market, and it was seeing "this life, these colors that change from week to week" that convinced her to try her hand at running a business.

These days, Dafne generally creates floral arrangements for weddings, from table centerpieces to bridal bouquets. She enjoys creating a personalized world for each couple and for every atmosphere, always favoring seasonal plants. She has also done a lot of work for photoshoots and film sets, and takes great pleasure in conjuring arrangements she would like to receive as a gift herself.

Back in her workshop, she tells us that every flower has its own personality and particular symbolism, especially in Mexico; she would never use *cempasúchiles* (Mexican marigolds) for a wedding, for example, as they are used to decorate altars to celebrate the Day of the Dead, and their petals are said to allow souls to return to earth. She goes on to say that all flowers are beautiful in some way

and no flower is ugly. "It's only the way we think about it that can be ugly." People tend to turn their noses up at red roses these days, for example, but Dafne is taking great delight in bringing them back in new ways.

Her aim when working on a bouquet is to bring it to life, telling a story that involves the people giving and receiving the gift, along with the person creating it. She plays with all five senses and likes to design arrangements that people want to taste, smell, and keep forever. She tells us that nothing makes her happier than a customer seeing her bouquets and asking: "Is that a pomegranate? Is that a branch from a pear tree? I had no idea you could use them like that…" The sky is the limit for Dafne and she gets her inspiration from the producers themselves, from their stories and her encounters with them.

Each bouquet tells the story of an encounter, the most beautiful of which was undoubtedly her encounter with Doña Gloria, the self-styled soul of the Mercado Jamaica; this elderly lady, as elegant as she is cheerful, has a thousand anecdotes about the flowers, plants, and shrubs she has been cultivating, harvesting, and selling for more than sixty years.

There is a flower for every occasion
in Mexico, allowing Dafne to dream up
endless arrangements.

EPHEMERAL BEAUTY

Dafne goes to the Mercado Jamaica every week to
pick out the best seasonal produce.

ABOVE

A xoloitzcuintle; *the name of this hairless dog (which is native to Mexico)
harks back to the Aztec god Xolotl.*

OPPOSITE

*The Conchita chapel in the square of the same name was the first
religious building constructed in Mexico City.*

NATURE

XOCHIMILCO ET ARCA TIERRA

THE CANALS OF MEXICO CITY

Xochimilco (pronounced *so-chi-mil-co*, meaning "field of flowers" in Nahuatl) lies in the far south of the city, more than 12 miles (20 km) from the city center. The lake here has been listed as a UNESCO World Heritage site since 1987 and is in fact all that remains of the ancient lake of Texcoco, around which the Aztecs constructed Tenochtitlan, their capital.

You may hear Mexicans mention the "Venice of Mexico" or "floating gardens" but Xochimilco is far more than just a tourist attraction. It is a cultural, social, and historical example of crop cultivation on artificial islands and of genuine Aztec heritage. Xochimilco ecological park is also home to one of the world's rarest amphibians; the axolotl is a species of salamander about 8in (20 cm) long that supports an entire thousand-year-old ecosystem almost single-handedly.

Some 252 miles (406 km) of canals crisscross the 30,000 acres (12,000 ha) of the Xochimilco site and visitors can explore an agricultural technique here that is unique to Mexico; *chinampas* are artificial islands (made up of a mixture of roots and plants) that are laid out as fields under constant irrigation. They only way to see them up close is to take a *trajinera*, one of the long skiffs that glide over the turbid waters of Xochimilco.

There are in fact two Xochimilcos; one is colorful and festive, with plenty of alcohol, revelry, and loud music, and every teenager will have a fuzzy memory of their first outing on the canals, often coinciding with their first beer (and their first hangover). The other is symbolized by the Arca Tierra project, which aims to enable the *chinampas* to continue to produce excellent vegetables even though more than eighty percent of them have now been abandoned and left to lie fallow. Arca Tierra also promotes interaction between farmers, artisans, and foodies, and a collective of more than thirty famous Mexican chefs have been working together to breathe new life into one of the capital's most iconic areas, at once preserving tradition and conserving the environment.

You need to rise early to get the most out of the Xochimilco experience; the canals awaken slowly at dawn, just as the sun is rising, revealing a magical and mystical landscape.

Arca Tierra begins to
reveal its charms
at sunrise.

Xochimilco is best explored
by boat, gliding down
the canals.

The irrigation system used for the
chinampas is found nowhere else
in the world and revolutionized
Mexican agriculture.

Arca Tierra provides
ongoing training and
apprenticeships.

Arca Tierra organizes intimate
lunch parties and cooking
workshops.

Xochimilco is used
both for pasture
and agriculture.

Cempasúchiles (Mexican
marigolds) are grown directly
on the *chinampas*.

Dawns turns the
artificial canals
to gold.

You can take a party tour of
the canals from the jetties
in Xochimilco.

A cow grazing on a chinampa *in Xochimilco. The volcanoes of Iztaccíhuatl and Popocatépetl are just visible in the background.*

MERCADO JAMAICA

MARCHÉ AUX FLEURS

The Mercado Jamaica, the capital's largest
flower market, is a city within a city.

WHOLESALE

Professional traders meet on Fridays to organize the weekend's deliveries.

MEXICO VALLEY

Producers come from far and wide to supply the market.

WORKING ACROSS THE GENERATIONS

Some of the same families have worked in the market for more than a hundred years.

EVENTS

Birthdays or weddings, there are flowers for every occasion.

FLORAL CREATIONS

All kinds of arrangements are available, from funeral wreaths to table centerpeices.

MEXICAN MARIGOLDS

The market is taken over by orange flowers in October; *cempasúchiles* are in season.

RELIGION

The Easter holidays are a busy season for the market.

EXOTIC FLOWERS

If you are looking for something special, the Mercado Jamaica is the place to go.

ABOVE

A cempasúchile *(Mexican marigold) seller exhibiting his wares from
the back of a truck during the All Souls' Day celebrations.*

OPPOSITE

*A lime-washed wall stained with ocher on one of the area's
pedestrianized streets.*

ABOVE

Garbage collectors sort domestic trash right on the street.

OPPOSITE

Tortillas *are at the heart of Mexican food and there is a* tortillería
on every street corner.

DÍA DE MUERTOS

"The cult of life, however profound and absolute it may be,
is also a death cult; the two are inseparable. A civilization that denies
death will end up denying life as well," wrote Octavio Paz,
one of Mexico's most influential authors, in his iconic
The Labyrinth of Solitude of 1950.

Few have summed up the Mexican relationship with death as well as Octavio Paz, who won the Nobel Prize for Literature in 1990. Death may cause tears and sadness across large parts of the planet, but in Mexico, it is celebrated with dancing and drinking, and marked with flowers and festivities.

The Day of the Dead, which commemorates the return of the departed to the world of the living in a celebration of life, is filled with a mysticism that sparks curiosity and fascination in many other cultures. It is a tradition that challenges and raises questions in equal measure, and its origins remain nebulous and mysterious. The current consensus among anthropologists is that the indigenous tribes of Latin America celebrated their dead for months on end, although some (such as France's Georges Bataille) have also suggested that pre-Columbian civilizations accompanied these religious ceremonies with human sacrifice.

Thousands of years later, Mexicans still decorate altars to remember and honor those who have passed away, surrounding photos of the deceased with arrangements of *cempasúchiles* (Mexican marigolds) – orange flowers said to show the souls of the deceased the path to those who love them and remember them. The altars are also often piled up with the favorite foods of those who can no longer eat them, including *pan de muerto*, a round pastry made with orange blossom and sprinkled with sugar; the crossed strips of pastry on top are supposed to represent two bones.

Over the years, the Day of the Dead has become an unmissable date in the diary for Mexicans and foreigners alike, and families in the most traditional villages will gather in the cemetery on All Souls to eat and drink with their deceased friends and relatives. It is not uncommon for complete strangers to invite you to join them, and they will take great delight in telling you the funniest and most moving stories about their loved ones.

The *Día de Muertos* parade popularized in the James Bond movie *Spectre* blends pre-Columbian traditions and tropes with more recent ideas, such as the image of Catrina, a popular character dreamed up by Mexican printmaker José Guadalupe Posada (to embody death, in fact).

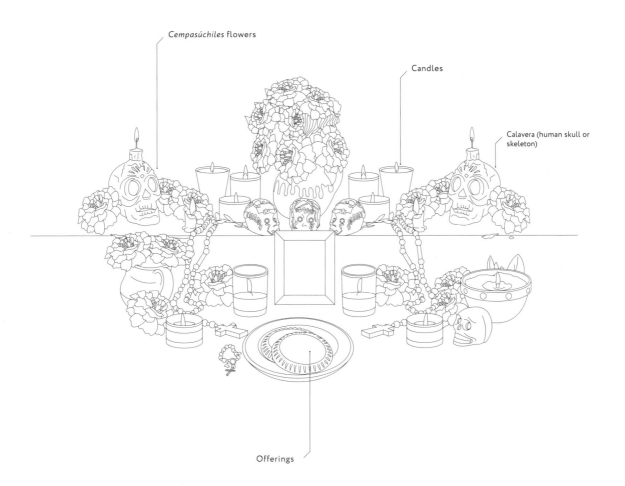

A DÍA DE MUERTOS ALTAR

Cempasúchiles flowers

Candles

Calavera (human skull or skeleton)

Offerings

IN MÉMORY OF THE DEAD

Mexican families set about creating altars on All Souls so that those who have died are never forgotten. The altars are decorated with *cempasúchile* flowers, photos, and the favorite foods and drinks of the deceased.

ABOVE

Mexico City's organilleros *will play their barrel organs*
for you for a few coins.

OPPOSITE

Unlike the rest of the city, Coyoacán's streets are more
densely vegetated than its gardens.

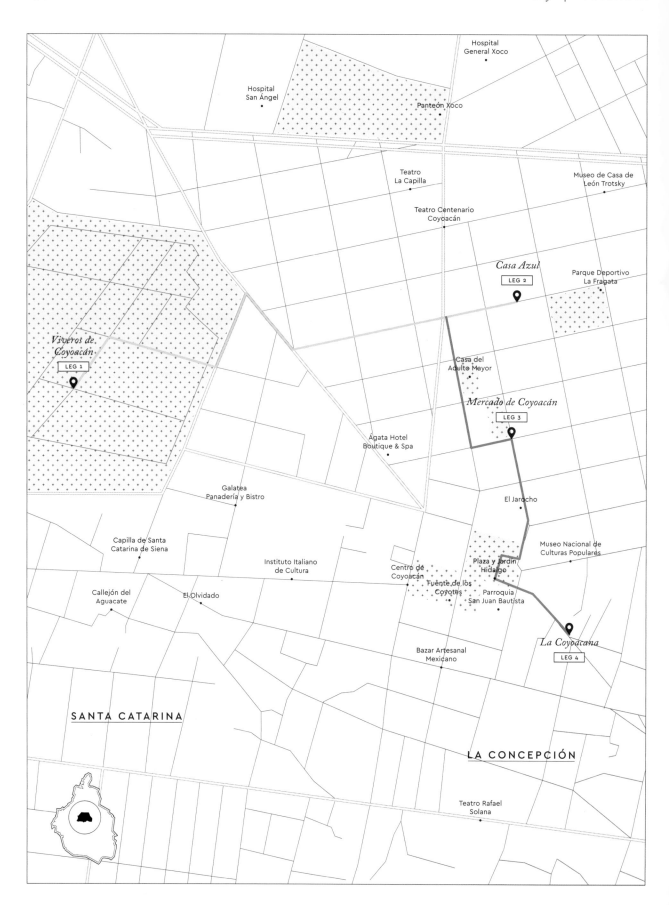

Hospital
General Xoco

Hospital
San Ángel

Panteón Xoco

Teatro
La Capilla

Museo de Casa de
León Trotsky

Teatro Centenario
Coyoacán

Casa Azul
LEG 2

Parque Deportivo
La Fragata

*Viveros de
Coyoacán*
LEG 1

Casa del
Adulto Mayor

Mercado de Coyoacán
LEG 3

Ágata Hotel
Boutique & Spa

Galatea
Panadería y Bistro

El Jarocho

Capilla de Santa
Catarina de Siena

Museo Nacional de
Culturas Populares

Instituto Italiano
de Cultura

Centro de
Coyoacán

Plaza y Jardín
Hidalgo

Callejón del
Aguacate

El Olvidado

Fuente de los
Coyotes

Parroquia
San Juan Bautista

La Coyoacana
LEG 4

Bazar Artesanal
Mexicano

SANTA CATARINA

LA CONCEPCIÓN

Teatro Rafael
Solana

A TRANQIL AND AUTHENTIC VILLAGE

Coyoacán keeps the flame of Frida Kahlo's memory alive and Casa Azul,
the artist's home and studio, is one of the country's most popular museums.
The area has so much more to offer, however.

LEG 1: A NATURE BATH

Athletes gather for an early morning rendezvous in Viveros de Coyoacán, a 1,440-acre (584-ha) park that forms a bubble of biodiversity in the heart of the capital. Others come here to visit the plant sellers that supply the city with greenery of every kind (cactuses, palm trees, succulents).

LEG 2: EXPLORING A COLONIAL VILLAGE

The cobbled streets and basalt walls hark back to a distant past when Coyoacán was no more than a village. Although the area has long since been swallowed up by urban sprawl, it still retains its bohemian charm and it's easy to get lost as you make your way between craft sellers and street artists. Having enjoyed a delicious grilled *elote* (corn on the cob) slathered in mayonnaise and chili powder, join the line in the shade of the eucalyptus trees in front of Casa Azul, the house/museum where Frida Kahlo spent the majority of her life.

LEG 3: TRADITION AND TOURISM AT THE MARKET

If you need to recalibrate your senses, nothing beats a trip to the Mercado de Coyoacán, a market seemingly frozen in time, where you can sample some lesser known varieties of fruit and vegetables, pick up a handmade *piñata*, or pluck up the courage to try some *chapulines* (toasted, salted grasshoppers) or *sal de gusano* (agave worm salt). The main attraction, however, is its selection of *tostadas* (thin and crispy, toasted corn *tortillas*), which are made to order and filled with a topping of your choice (cod or shrimp ceviche, chicken *mole* sauce, or pork crackling), washed down with an *agua de sabor*, a drink flavored with seasonal fruit.

LEG 4: HOT CHOCOLATE

Take the Calle Ignacio Allende up toward Coyoacán's old cathedral, following the crowds and the scent in the air, and you will find yourself stopping right outside El Jarocho.

Since 1953, this small café has been serving up a hundred percent Mexican coffee and hot chocolate made with water or milk in the purest *chiapaneca* ("from the state of Chiapas") tradition using a *molinillo*, a kind of pre-Columbian whisk made of wood – so delicious with some *churros* sprinkled with cinnamon sugar! Continue on toward Plaza Hidalgo and the Fuente de los Coyotes, where the terraces and restaurants opposite San Juan Bautista church fill up in the evenings, and don't even think of leaving without calling in to La Coyoacana, one of the most famous cantinas in the country, where it would be rude not to try some tequilas and share some typical Mexican food.

BIOGRAPHIES

Thibaut Mommalier was born in Évry in 1992 and discovered Mexico at the age of fifteen on a school exchange. Having had a career as a designer/editor in advertising, he left Paris to settle in Ciudad de México in 2017, where he teaches French language and culture. Having fallen in love with Mexico, its culture and its cuisine, he takes advantage of every opportunity and encounter to try to share its soul and understand its subtleties.

Franck Juery is a freelance photographer mainly working in publishing, the music industry, journalism, communications, and advertising. In his commissioned work, he strives to capture his subjects associatively by working with images that inform one another within the scope of a narrative, or simply through dreamlike and poetic juxtapositions.

PHOTOGRAPHIC CREDITS

All the photographs in this book are by Franck Juery, with the exception of: ©Kurimanzutto/Onnis Luque: 107, bottom right. © Barragan Foundation, Switzerland/Adagp, Paris, 2024: 107, 112. The editor has taken every care to secure the rights for the various elements within this volume, but should the book contain any aspect infringing upon the rights of third parties, they are invited to contact the publishers.

First published in English
in 2025 by Rizzoli Universe UK,
an imprint of Rizzoli International Publications,
Somerset House, West Wing
Strand
London WC2R 1LA
www.rizzoliusa.com

Originally published in French in 2024 as
Petit Atlas Hédoniste – Mexico
by Éditions du Chêne – Hachette Livre

www.editionsduchene.fr

Copyright © 2024 Éditions du Chêne

For Rizzoli
Publisher: Charles Miers
Editor: Vicky Orchard

For Éditions du Chêne
Editor-in-chief: Emmanuel Le Vallois
Artistic Director: Sabine Houplain

A CIP catalogue record for this book is available from the British Library.

ISBN 9780789345790

2025 2026 2027 / 10 9 8 7 6 5 4 3 2 1

Printed in China

Visit us online:
Instagram.com/RizzoliBooks
Facebook.com/RizzoliNewYork
X: @Rizzoli_Books
Youtube.com/user/RizzoliNY